Also available in this series

CANDLEMAKING
JEWELLERY
POTTERY
APPLIQUE
FRAMING
SOFT TOYS Book 1
MACRAME
CROCHET
RUGMAKING
WEAVING
MORE SOFT TOYS
COUNTRY CRAFTS
THE ART OF DRIED AND PRESSED FLOWERS
FILOGRAPHY
BARGELLO
FURNITURE MAKING
CHILDREN'S CLOTHES
HOME DECORATION

METRIC CONVERSION TABLE

INCHES		MILLIMETRES
1/4	=	6
1/2	=	13
3/4	=	19
1	=	25
2	=	51
3	=	76
4	=	102
5	=	127
6	=	152
7	=	178
8	=	203
9	=	229
10	=	254

gifts

PAMELA RODWAY

illustrated by Laura Potter
photography by Richard Sharpe Studios

PAN BOOKS LTD
LONDON AND SYDNEY

First published 1974 by Sampson Low
This edition published 1975 by Pan Books Ltd,
Cavaye Place, London SW10 9PG

Printed in Spain
ISBN 0 330 24484 1

CONTENTS

INTRODUCTION

It's a strange but true phenomenon that it always seems to be 'gift-giving' time! Birthdays appear to crop up at least once every month, as do weddings and new babies! There's always a 'grannie' who appreciates it so much if you take her some little thing when you go to see her, and of course—Christmas—which would seem to come round much more often than just once a year! Heart-warming though it is to give presents to friends and loved ones, it does become a costly business, increasingly so as even the simplest little ornamental items cost more each time you see them in the shops.

The only practical and by far the most satisfactory solution is to make gifts yourself. After all a carefully thought out present, which you have taken the trouble to make is an infinitely more precious and exciting thing to receive than a mass-produced shop-bought item, however exotic it is. Men and women alike have so much more scope for making presents truly personal if they make them themselves.

In this book we have given ideas for gifts for everyone—young couples moving into their first home together, teenagers in need of practical items or merely a mascot to encourage them through those endless exams, and of course something 'for the man who has everything'.

All techniques used are simple and thoroughly 'step-by-step' explained, so there's simply no excuse for those with the time-worn cry of 'I'm no good with my hands—I can't make anything!' There are things that both men and women will enjoy making, giving and receiving.

Collect all the necessary items together, (clearly listed under 'You Will Need') for each project before embarking on any single project. We have given precise lists of the things we used, but the nice thing about these ideas is that they are all open to your own interpretation, so they become truly your ideas. You are unlikely to choose for example, exactly the same material for the patchwork presents on page 12 or the same dried flowers or container for the beautiful shelf arrangement on page 36. You will probably want to draw up your own design for the bagatelle board on page 34; and the kind of collage pictures you create, whilst following our instructions on page 20, will intrinsically contain your own personal touch depending on the bits and pieces you use and the subject you choose to depict. It all adds up to more fun, more scope, more exciting presents and more money in your pocket!

The Gift Of Light

In Scandinavia, the giving of a candle is known as 'a gift of light'—a lovely sentiment which goes far in explaining the popularity of candles as presents. They are easy and rewarding to make, and even your first attempts will look professional. Make them plain, multi-coloured, stripey, marbled or intricately patterned. You don't need elaborate or expensive equipment for any of them, and there's lots and lots of scope for you to exercise your imagination and creativity.

YOU WILL NEED:
Candle wax
Candle dyes
Stearin (to make the candle opaque)
Wicks of 3 thicknesses
Sealing compound of Plasticine
Wick rods (or skewers, cocktail sticks, etc.)
Various moulds (bought or improvised from household containers)
Double boiler
Tablespoon
Newspaper

Bought moulds come in rigid square, round, star and cone shapes, and in flexible rubber to give patterns in relief.

For an average-size plain candle, use wax and stearin in a ratio of 9 tablespoons to 1. For a 1 in. thick candle, use thin wick; for 2 in.– medium; and for 3 in. or more–thick. Melt wax in a double boiler, over a low heat.

Cut piece of wick 3 ins. longer than the mould. Dip it in melted wax. When it is dry, tie it to rod. Take pan off heat.

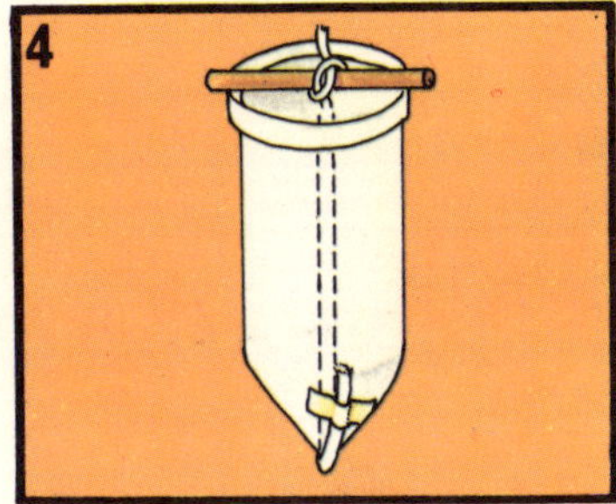

Thread wick through hole in bottom of mould. Pull down and fix to outside with adhesive tape. Rod should rest on mould.

Seal hole with Plasticine. Stand mould upright or support in cardboard tube or glass if using flexible mould.

Stand pan back on heat. Add 1 tablespoon stearin and wax dye ($\frac{1}{8}$ of a stick gives average colour).

Stir until mixed. Cool for a few minutes and pour to top of mould. Leave remaining wax in pan. Tap mould to free bubbles.

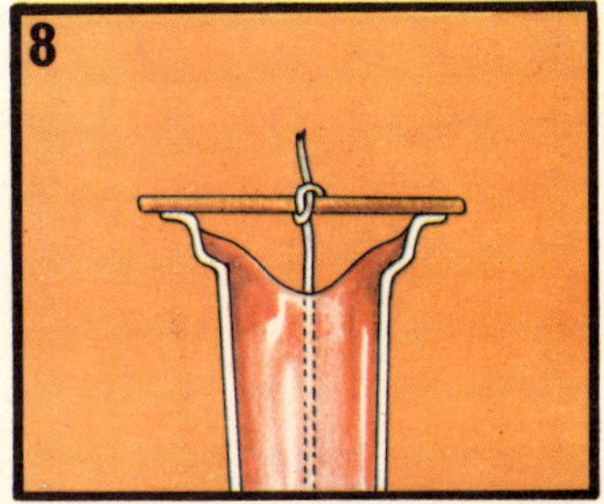

As depressions form in candle top, break surface wax and top up with hot wax. Repeat as necessary and leave to cool.

Remove seal and tape. Tap rigid mould to release candle. Trim wick.

To release candle from flexible mould, rub mould with soapy hands and peel back from candle. 'Polish' candle with a soft cloth and carefully wash and dry mould ready for re-use.

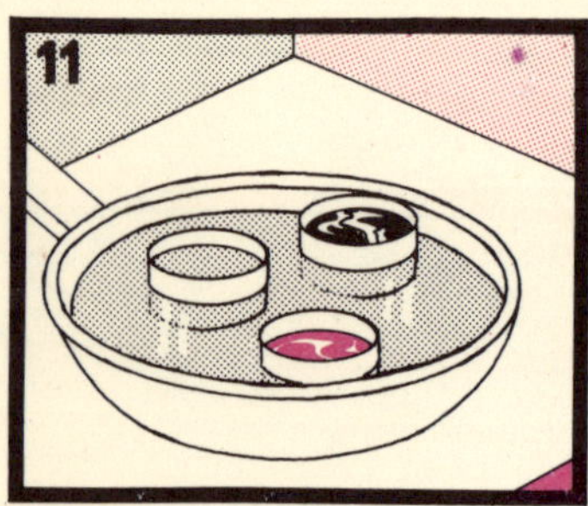

For multi-coloured candles, melt quantities of wax in separate pots. Add stearin and dyes. Stand pots in hot water.

For a 2-colour candle, prepare mould and half fill with one colour wax. When firm, fill with second colour wax.

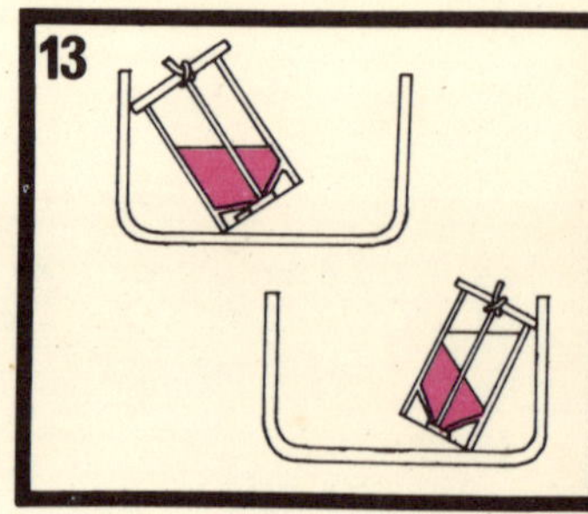

To make diagonal stripes, tilt mould with wax as shown. Support until each colour solidifies, then pour in new colour.

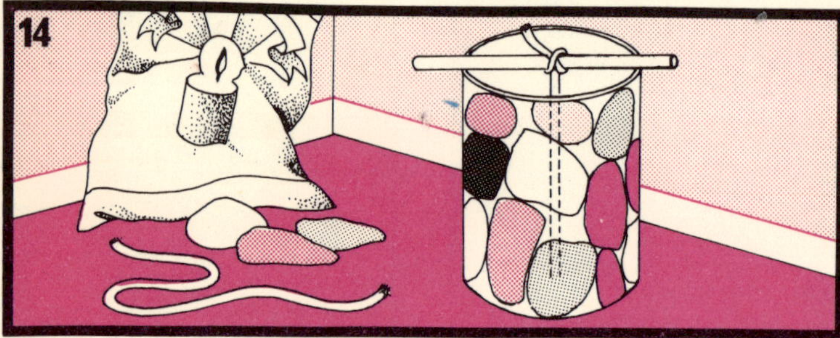

For 'chunks' candles, set wick and fill mould with coloured chunks of cold wax, pressing them against mould sides. Fill up with white or coloured wax. Tap to release air bubbles and leave to set.

For a 'marbled' candle, almost fill mould with wax and leave until skin forms. Run different coloured wax on top and pierce at intervals with a skewer so upper wax runs down through candle. Mix around slightly with skewer each time.

To give unusual texture, make up coloured wax and leave in bowl to cool. Whip with a whisk and pour into mould.

For an attractive effect, set candle in a wine glass. Warm the glass first. These candles can be safely burnt in the glass.

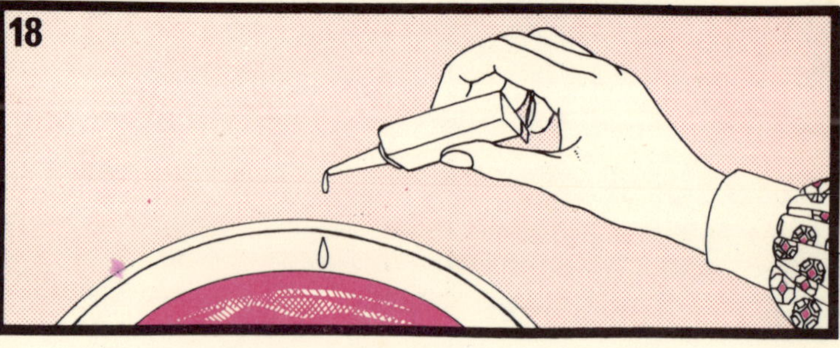

For scented candles—add a few drops of candle perfume (available from craft shops) to wax—but use sparingly!

Improvise moulds. Use cream cartons taped together, mousse pots, cups, glasses, etc. Make sure candle can be released without breaking the container–it should be larger at the top. Secure wick to bottom of container with spot of wax.

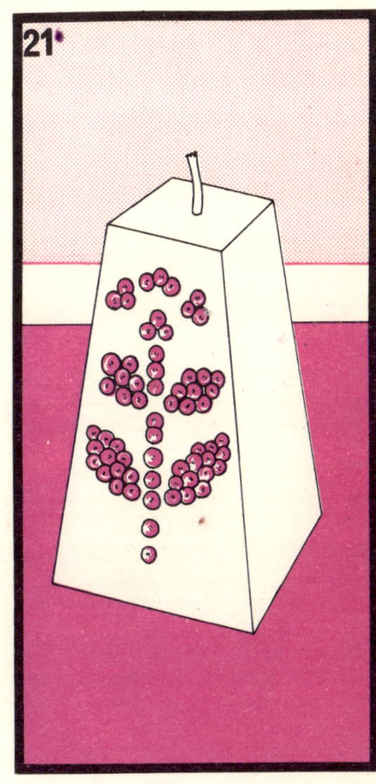

Decorate plain candles with sequins (plastic ones melt down as they get hot).

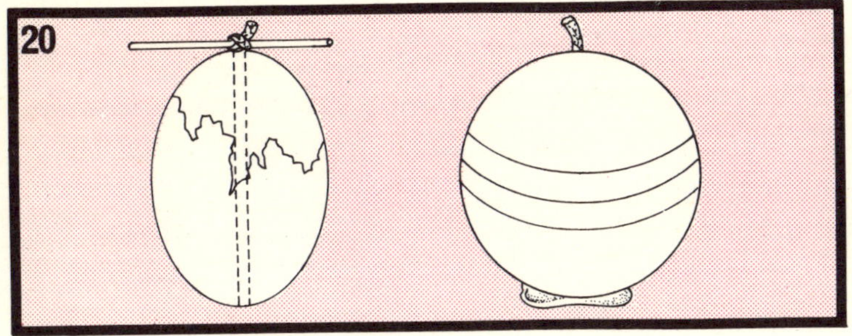

Easter candles: Blow egg and thread waxed wick through. Seal pointed end. Fill with wax using tiny funnel. Break shell when set.

Decorate a cone candle with sequins in a spiral shape. Run a thread of household adhesive round candle and attach sequins.

Use guipure daisies to decorate base of candles. Remove as candle burns down.

Accentuate a moulded pattern by picking it out in metallic paint applied with a fine brush.

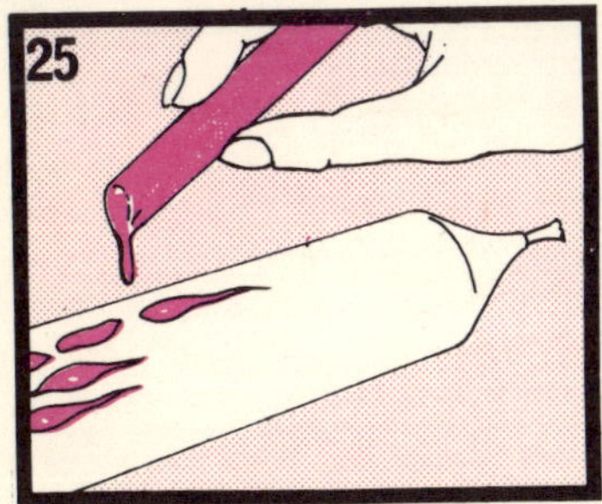

Wax crayons melted over a match or candle flame can effectively decorate a plain, slim candle (even a plain household one).

DO pour wax when really hot, and cool gradually. Make sure wick size is correct or flame may be smoky or drowned.

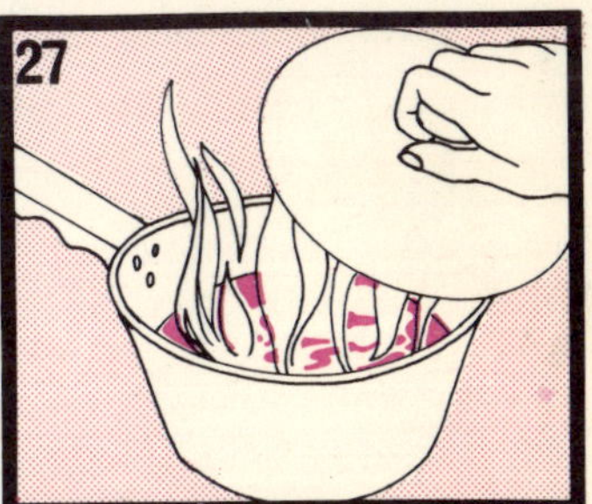

DON'T melt wax over direct heat or it may catch fire. If this happens, smother with pan lid. DON'T get water in melting wax.

Patchwork Presents

Patchwork trimming adds a personal touch to a whole range of gifts for the home. As a house-warming present, perhaps, here is a roller blind, tablecloth and cushion set—although any one of these would be acceptable on its own. Choose cottons which are closely-woven and about the same weight. Wash if needed, and iron before use. A motif of a number of patches forming a square is infinitely adaptable. It is shown here as 4 squares in a block, as a cushion; 4 squares in a row on the edge of a blind; and 20 squares bordering a tablecloth. The more industrious could make a complete cloth with 36 squares. Hand sewing, is, of course, traditional for pieceing patchwork, but a machine can be used for making up the soft furnishings. The squares can be applied to the hem of a straight or gathered long skirt, on a waistcoat, on curtains—almost anywhere.

YOU WILL NEED:
For patchwork:
Remnants of closely-woven cotton
Pieces of card for templates
Needle–thread–scissors
Pencil–rule–(steam) iron
For tablecloth:
36 in. sq. plain cotton fabric
For cushions:
13 in. sq. plain cotton fabric
Press stud tape or zip
For roller blind:
Roller blind kit
Saw–screwdriver–hammer
Tacks
Fabric to fit window (either plastic, or cotton with lining)
Lathe–the width of window

The rising star is a traditional pattern of 'pieces' patchwork, popular in Victorian times. As shown in the scale drawing above, it requires 33 patches. It can, however, be simplified by substituting a single square for the 7 patches in the centre motif.

The emphasis can be changed by varying use of materials. (See Nos. 2 and 3.)

A pink floral motif in the centre is framed by toning colours.

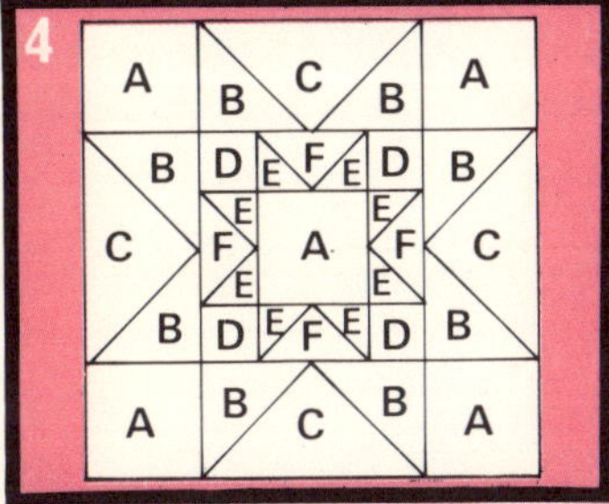

The templates. For complete design cut 5 of square (A), 8 of triangle (B), 4 of triangle (C), 4(D), 8(E), and 4 of triangle (F).

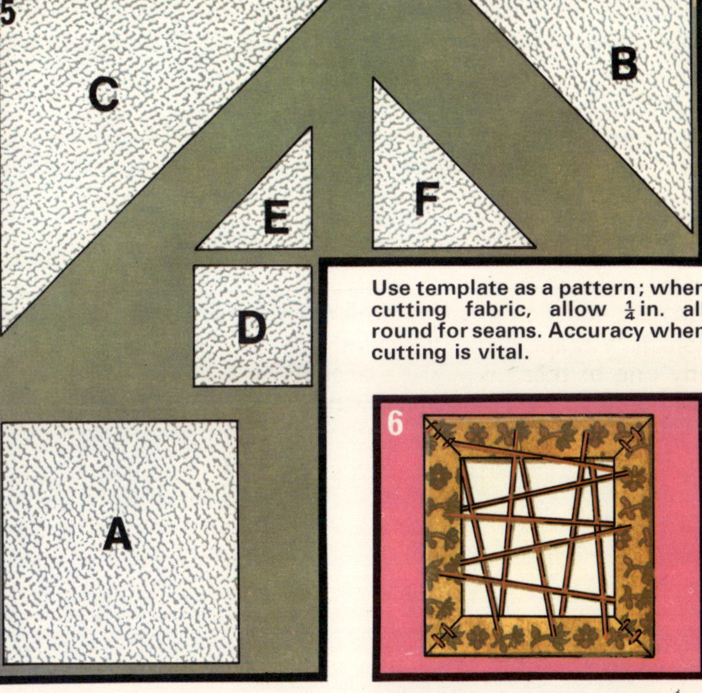

Use template as a pattern; when cutting fabric, allow $\frac{1}{4}$ in. all round for seams. Accuracy when cutting is vital.

To centre the design of a patterned fabric, cut a template with a 'window' the size of the patch and move about on fabric.

6

Turn $\frac{1}{4}$ in. seam allowance to back of template, mitre and sew corners, sew large stitches criss-cross to secure and tighten.

Join the patches together at the back with tiny hemming or over-sewing stitches. Start by joining the pieces to the centre square and continue working the pattern outwards.

Leave templates in place until all outside edges are sewn. Then cut the tacking to release them.

Back 1 6 in. square with plain fabric and fill with pot-pourri. Oversew edge to make a small scented cushion.

Join 4 of the 6 in. squares to make a larger cushion. Back with plain material again, leaving one side unstitched.

Finish off open edge with press studs or a zip, so cushion can be easily removed and the cover washed.

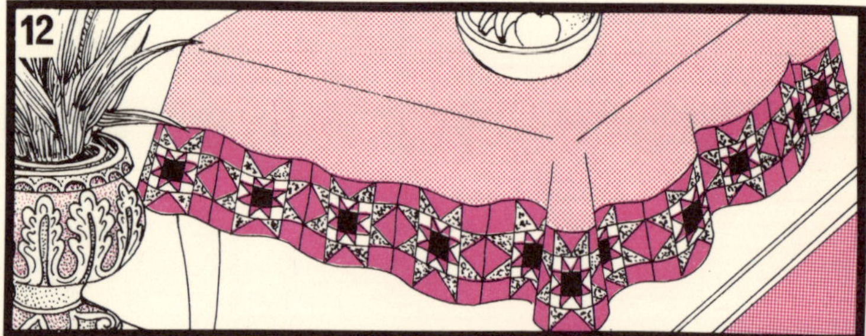

To make a tablecloth 3 ft. square, make up 20 of the basic 6 in. square patches. Appliqué these round the edge of a square cloth in a toning colour.

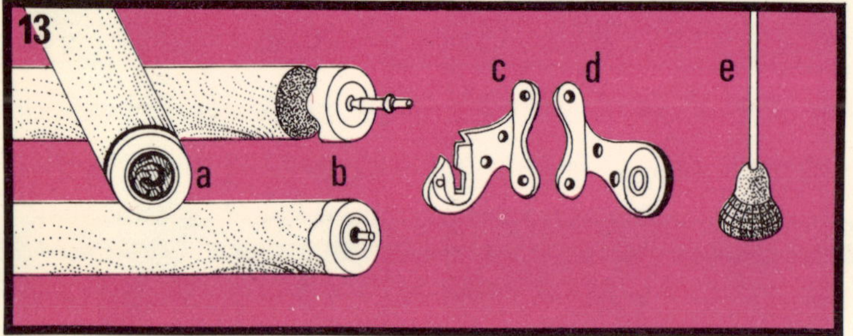

Buy a roller blind kit to fit the window. There will be a wooden roller with rectangular pin and spring fitting at one end (a); an end cap and spindle to fit on the other (b); metal brackets (c, d); and an 'acorn set'–the pull cord (e).

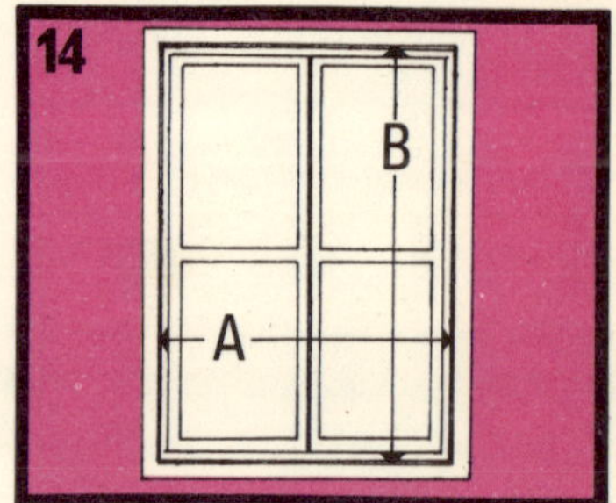

Measure window for fabric width (A) and length (B). Allow extra 5 ins. at top to cover roller, and 2 ins. at bottom.

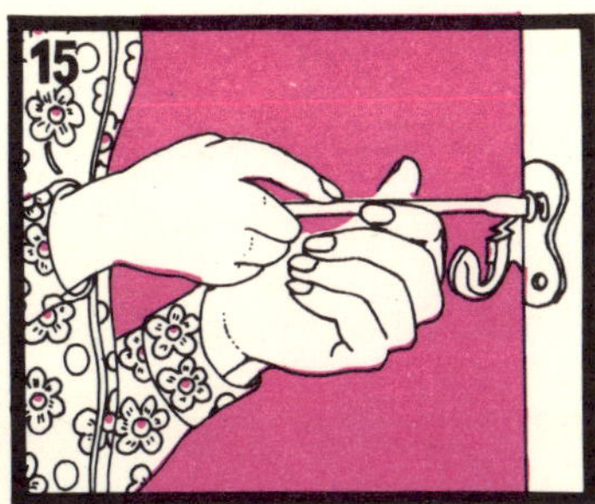

Fix brackets. Screw flanges flat against frame (not moving part). Measure from sill to ensure brackets are parallel.

Cut fabric to width of roller. If you have to use fabric narrower than window, join widths in centre. Press seams open.

If using cotton fabric, choose an interlining. Iron on to wrong side of fabric; avoid making creases on the face.

Turn $\frac{1}{2}$ in. at sides to wrong side. Press and slipstitch to lining. Turn under $\frac{1}{2}$ in. at bottom; press; turn $1\frac{1}{2}$ ins. more and machine.

Add second row of stitching close to hem edge to complete channel for lathe. Cut lathe to right length to fit.

How you arrange the patchwork motifs will depend on width of blind. If it is a multiple of 6 ins., use squares in a strip.

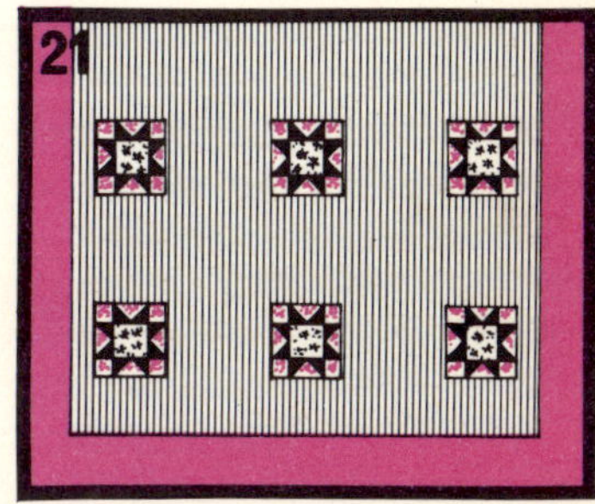

Alternatively, use the central motif only, which gives 3 in. multiples, or a random pattern of the patchwork designs.

Make up the squares of patches. Sew together if a border is wanted. Oversew or slipstitch squares to front of blind.

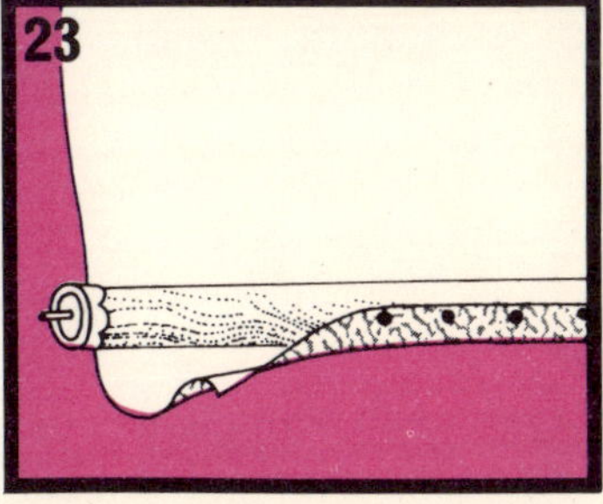

At top, press fabric $\frac{1}{2}$ in. to right side. Pass behind roller, wrong side out and tack.

Insert lathe. Place blind in brackets and screw on pull cord (instructions in kit).

Beautiful Bottles

Bottle presents are really ideal for everyone—both to give and to receive. They are imaginative, original and amusing—as well as practical and economical! Start saving 'empties' and practise decorating them with ordinary lacquer and trimming. To begin with, transform jam jars into pencil holders for children; mustard pots into useful herb jars, and wine bottles into dramatic ornaments. Then try your hand at some ideas of your own.

YOU WILL NEED:
A selection of bottles and jars
White spirit
Kitchen paper towel
Lacquer in different colours
$\frac{1}{2}$ in., $\frac{1}{4}$ in., and 1 or 2 smaller brushes
Household adhesive—sequins
Cut-out decorations—labels
Gold doyley etc.
Pencil and felt-tip pen.

Assemble bottles and painting materials. Thoroughly wash and dry bottles, and wipe over with white spirit to remove grease.

Plan designs for bottles, relating to shape, sketching if necessary. Decide on colours, decorations, labels, etc.

Unless painting inside the bottle, apply an undercoat of neutral-coloured lacquer. This will give a better finish.

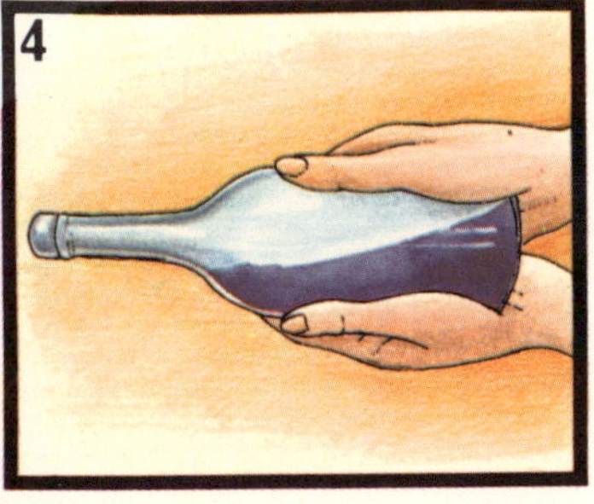

Bottles may be painted inside by pouring in paint and turning bottle until coated. Pour out excess paint.

Bottles which lend themselves to imaginative designs include tall disinfectant bottles, ordinary jam jars, hock bottles, Mateus Rose bottles and mustard pots.

Tall disinfectant bottle is painted blue inside (see no. 4). Pattern in glass casts shadows on interior painted surface.

Jam jars with faces make fun pen-tidies for children. Undercoat in pink, draw face on in pencil as a painting guide.

A hock bottle makes a romantic 'sailor's Valentine'! Paint bottle pink, stick on gilt doyley motifs and sequins.

Undercoat Mateus bottle; paint red. Draw pattern in felt tip, then paint design in black on alternate sections.

Black accentuates unusual shape of little spice jar. Decorate with gilt label and spots. Top may be painted or left same.

Paint moulded jar, gilt inside and stick little Victorian print where label was. Paint top black. Use for decoration only.

Join The Suede Brigade

These attractive suede cuff-links and watchstrap are very easy to make, even if you haven't worked with leather before. Smart and practical, they'll make very acceptable gifts. Choose an unusual colour of suede and either brass or silver studs—the kind which are used for studding denim (available from most large stores) would be suitable. Failing these, brass paper fasteners make a good substitute. The prongs, once pushed through the suede, may be cut off and the ends flattened down. Measurements given are for a watch $1\frac{1}{2}$ ins. by 1 in., with a strap holder width of $\frac{5}{8}$in. You will obviously need to measure the watch for which your strap is intended, and make slight size adjustments if necessary.

YOU WILL NEED:
Piece of suede approx. 8 ins. by 11 ins.
32 small denim studs or brass paper fasteners
Buckle $\frac{3}{4}$ in. wide
Pair cuff-link mounts
2 flat metal mounts 1 in. sq.
Copydex or other rubber-based adhesive
Ruler · razor blade · pencil
Skewer · small hammer ·
Kitchen paper towel

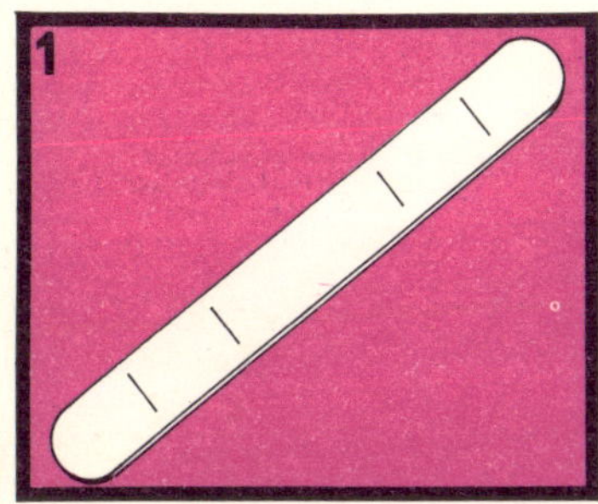

Cut 2 pieces of suede $6\frac{3}{4}$ ins. by $1\frac{1}{2}$ ins. and curve ends. Place wrong sides together and cut 4 slits right through.

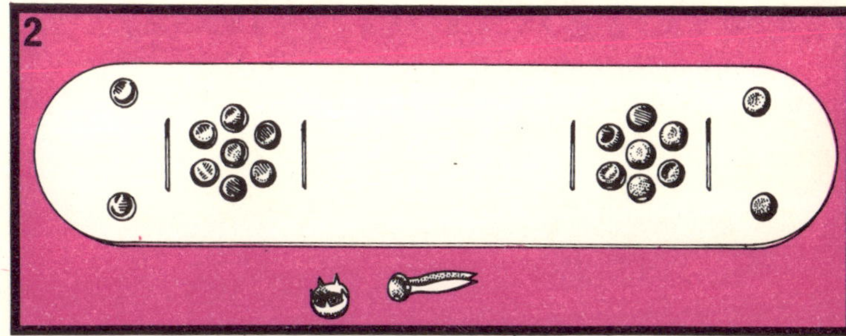

Place studs in pattern shown on 1 suede strip. Tap through with hammer, turn over and flatten points. Alternatively, use brass fasteners. Make small holes in the suede, push fasteners through, cut off points, then flatten.

Take other suede piece, trim a fraction off all round. Stick with adhesive to back of the studded pieces, matching slits.

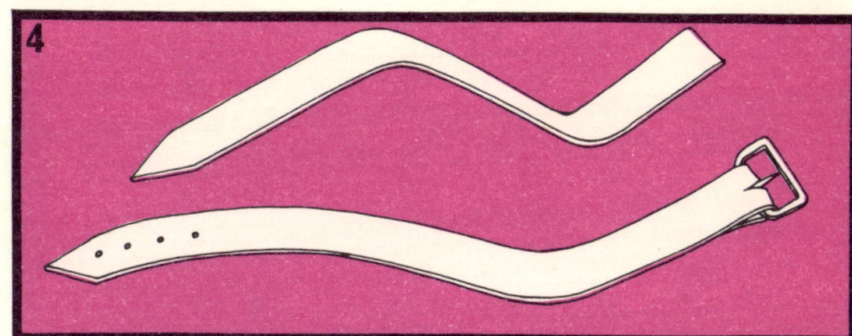

To make watch-holding strap, cut 2 suede pieces $10\frac{1}{2}$ ins. long and $\frac{1}{2}$ in. wide. Stick wrong sides together and point one end. Cut a small slit 1 in. from one end, and slip buckle through. Stick down suede end. Pierce 4 holes with skewer in other end.

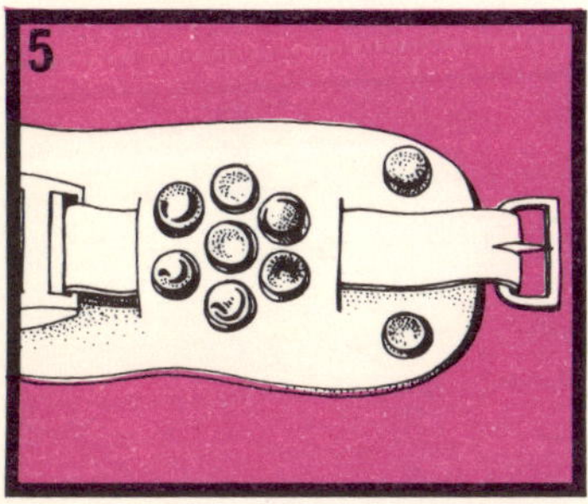

Thread strap through studded part, slotting on watch in middle. Stud pattern and width of main band can be varied.

To make the cuff-links, take a square metal mount and cut 2 pieces of suede about $\frac{1}{4}$ in. larger all round. On right sides carefully mark centre and 6 points round it, about $\frac{1}{2}$ in. away. Fix studs through these 7 points on each piece as before.

Turn pieces to wrong side; snip a square at each corner. Stick mount on centre. Turn over edges and stick down.

Cut two smaller squares of suede and stick on back to cover the raw edges and backs of studs. Allow to dry.

Stick cuff-link mounts in place with adhesive; leave to set. Be careful not to get adhesive on suede front.

Colourful Collage

Collage, the art of creating pictures from fabric, is the ideal craft for 'squirrels'. With a workbox full of bits and pieces, you have the makings of a gift that could hardly be more personal. Include, if you can, a snipping of a favourite old evening dress, her wedding dress or first kitchen curtains and give a friend a picture that is a joy to look at—and full of memories.

YOU WILL NEED:
1 piece of stiff card about 10 ins. by 15 ins., and 1 piece 2 ins. larger all round
Blue, green, brown, red and white fabric
Green wool, (boucle or mohair if possible)
Household foil
Grasses, motifs, etc. for trim
Glue, thread and hessian for mount
Copydex or other rubber-based adhesive

Assemble fabrics and trimmings, card and glue. First sketch picture to form a working guide. Collage pictures are fun presents if they relate directly to a friend's life—such as the boat shown.

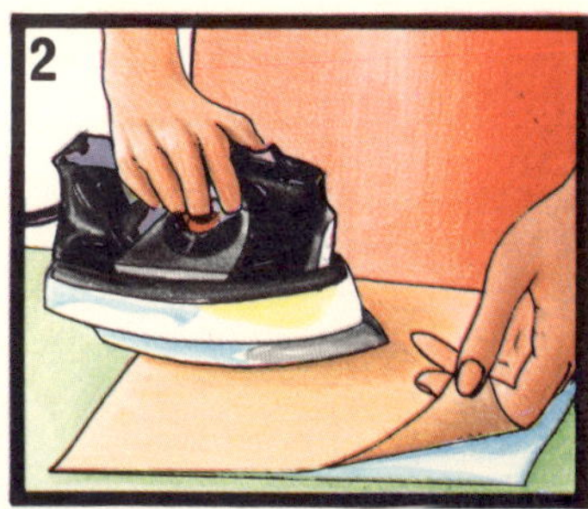

If material is likely to fray, apply piece of iron-on fabric backing before cutting. Cut background card to size.

Cut blue fabric for sky to come two-thirds down picture. Glue in place. Glue foil on remainder. Cut and add green foreground.

Cut brown tree trunk; glue along left of picture. Glue on lengths of green wool to represent leaves.

Cut hull in white, cabin in brown, sails in red. Cut mast and boom from ribbon; glue. Sew in cotton ribbon and pin man.

Using three shades of blue ric-rac braid, stick 'waves', mixing shades and allowing shine of silver foil to show through.

Add details of reeds, flowers, etc. using dried grass, guipure lace daisies or any other small cut-out decorative motif.

Cover larger piece of card with hessian; take hessian to back; mitre corners; and glue down.

Pin, sew or glue picture to backing to complete. If preferred, frame the picture in the usual way.

YOU WILL NEED:
Old picture frame and piece of stiff card to fit inside measurement
Steel · pencil · craft knife
Piece of closely-woven fabric approx. 2 ins. larger all round than card
Scissors. Needle and thread
A few tacks to secure backing into frame · Adhesive
Scraps of wool, mohair, brocade, linen, cotton and velvet
Scraps of fringe and bobble trimmings · Knitting wool
Guipure lace daisies and scrap of broderie anglaise
Flowers cut from dress or furnishing fabric

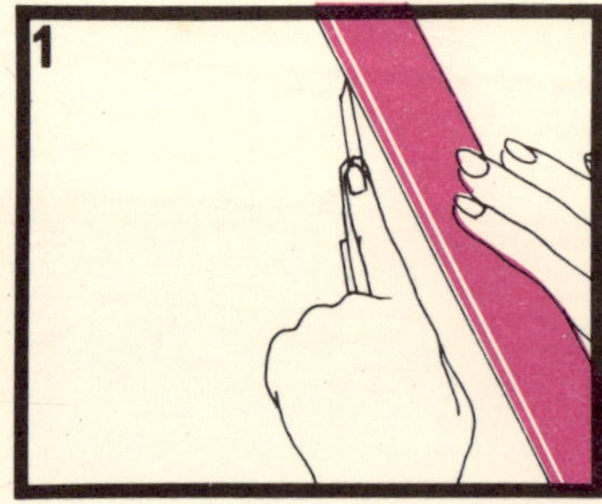

Accurately measure the inside of picture frame. Using steel rule and craft knife, cut card exactly to fit into frame.

Cut out background fabric approximately 2 ins. larger all round the card. Turn over the corners; oversew securely.

For an unwrinkled surface, take tiny running stitch along top edge, carry the thread to lower edge, and take another running stitch and draw thread tightly. Sew criss-cross in this way from top to bottom, and side to side, pulling tightly.

Start from centre of background. Cut piece of fabric $\frac{1}{8}$ of total area; spread adhesive sparingly; glue in place.

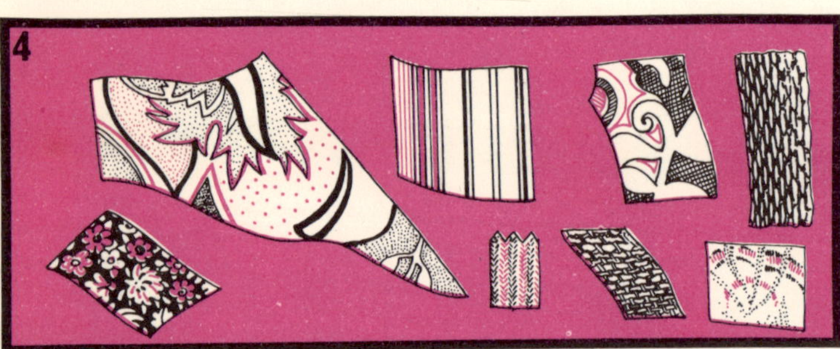

For a harmonised effect in the picture use contrasting textures and blending colours. Select a floral print and choose other fabrics in matching and toning colours. Cut into various shapes and sizes, using pinking shears for some pieces.

Having cut out a number of patches, place them on the background and move them around to achieve a pleasing balance.

Start glueing them in place. Overlap some. There is no need to keep lines straight or prevent fabric fraying.

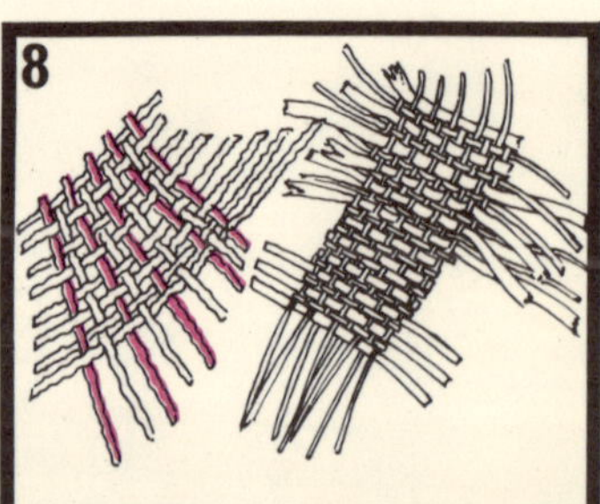

Select some materials (e.g. coarse lines and mohair) which are 'bad frayers' as these enhance the look. Pull them gently apart and overlay them on smooth fabrics.

Cut out and stick down flowers from fabric oddments, a motif from broderie Anglaise, and a piece of lace edging.

Continue building the picture outwards until you have covered most of the background, leaving a margin more or less all round.

Wind 12in. lengths of rug wool round finger; stick down. Fray mohair scrap each end; wind into roll; stick together at back.

Check that patch pieces look integrated and radiate from centre. Add final touches of frayed thread and trimmings.

Turn picture frame upside down; insert backing; secure with tacks along each side. Add hooks and picture cord if necessary.

Pebble Presents

Many of us can't resist collecting 'things' that appeal to us–particularly samples of Nature's handiwork. A day by the sea, for example, finds many of us fascinated by the pebbles on the beach. How perfectly smooth and beautifully shaped so many of them are . . . and by the time we have to pack up and head for home, a number of the 'best' stones have found their way into the beach bag. Convinced we'll find a use for them in the house, how often do they just get left lying around? Yet with little expense and just a few hours' work, those pebbles–and stones of all shapes and sizes–can be transformed with paint and varnish into attractive paperweights, door stops and 'worry beads' (pebbles to turn soothingly in the hand). Lovely, personal, but economical presents.

YOU WILL NEED:
Poster paints
Silver spray paint
Black Indian ink
Watercolour varnish
Methylated spirit
Brushes
Old toothbrush

Above is a selection of stones and pebbles we chose to decorate–copy our designs–or better still, make up your own to suit your stones.

Choose smooth, pleasingly shaped stone suitable for paperweights, worry beads or door stops. Wash and dry well.

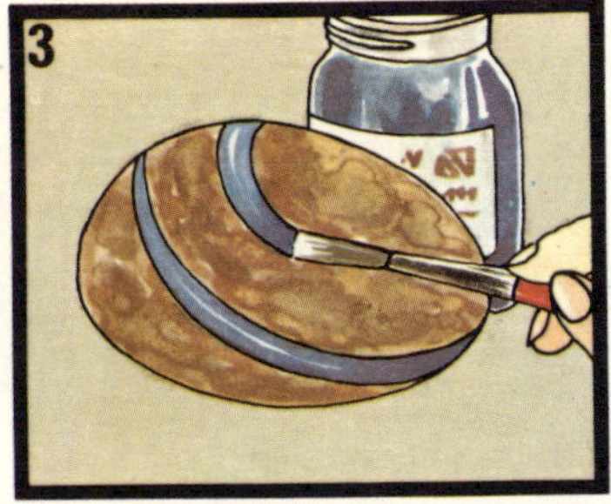

Draw designs in pencil or paint 'by eye'. If a design does not please you, you can wash if off before varnishing. Start again.

When stones are painted, varnish; brush on quickly in thin coat. Clean brushes in methylated spirit before varnish sets.

For triangles: Poster paint black lines. Allow to dry. Paint parallel lines and fill in between with contrasting colours.

For checked stones: paint stripes one way, cross with irregular ink stripes. Paint some sections different bright colours. For wavy lines stone, just paint irregular lines in poster paints.

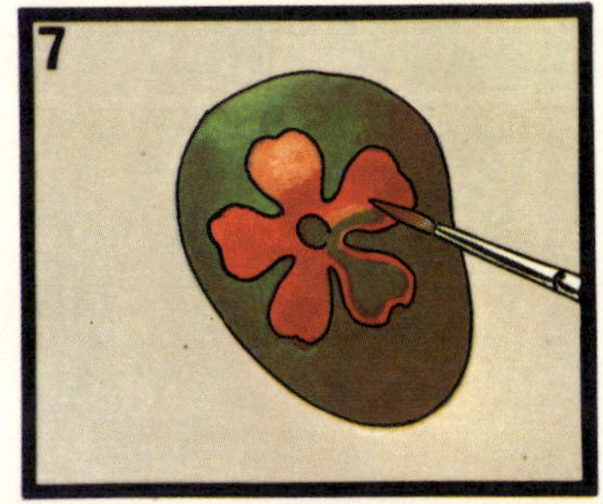

Flowers: paint stone all over. Leave to dry. Draw flower outline and fill in with paint. Varnish when dry.

For speckled stone: thin paints and ink. Put colours on one by one using a toothbrush. Stroke it with your thumb to spatter stone. Paint over stone. Varnish when dry. Try using silver spray paint too.

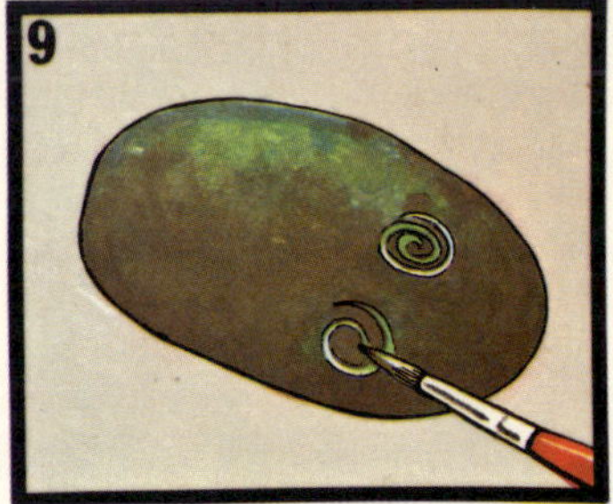

Paint 'eyes' on a stone. Paint stone all over with various colours. Paint 2 large circles at one end. Varnish.

Herb And Spice Basket

Here's an attractive method of storing herbs and spices—a natural rush basket! It is shallow enough to keep on a narrow kitchen shelf, although the 12 bright yellow tops make a gay splash of colour to keep beside you on a working surface. The jars are packed close together in the basket so the light won't get at the herbs and weaken the flavour. You can buy a bundle of rushes at most good craft shops. You will find that they are thick at the root end and taper off to almost nothing at the top. Cut from the base of the rushes to begin the check weave pattern and match them for thickness. Use the narrower ends for the pairing weave that goes round and round. Wipe each rush with a damp cloth before using, to clean and soften it, and then wipe again as you are working, to keep the material supple. You can, of course, copy the idea using jars of any size.

YOU WILL NEED:
A bundle of rushes
A box 12 ins. by 8 ins. to use as a mould
Scissors · piece of cloth · ruler
Blunt, large eyed needle
12 screw-top-jars (e.g. mustard jars, 2 ins. across at max. width, and approx. 2 ins. deep)
1 sheet of instant lettering (suggest Letraset sheet no. 227, 24pt Grotesque 7 type)

Cut 12 20 in. lengths and 14 18 in. lengths, all from thick end of rushes. Place longer ones close together on table.

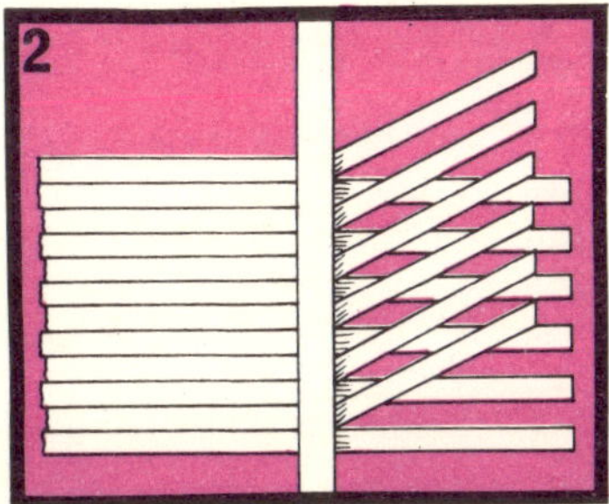

Lay ruler across the centre of rushes. Lift alternate ones, and insert an 18 in. rush between them and flat ones.

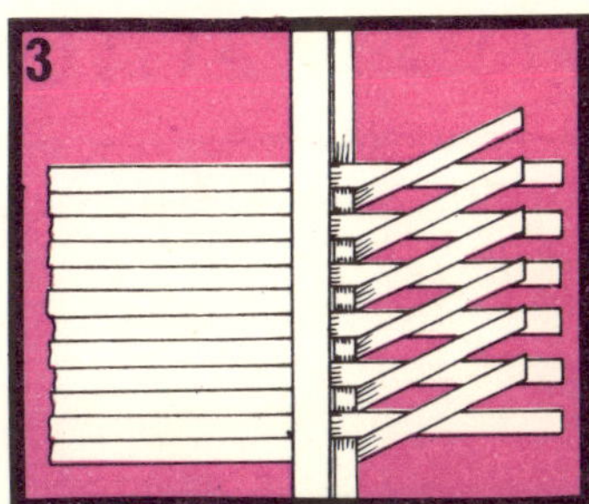

Now lift 'even-numbered' rushes, and place another rush under them. This will start lattice-effect, i.e. 'check weave'.

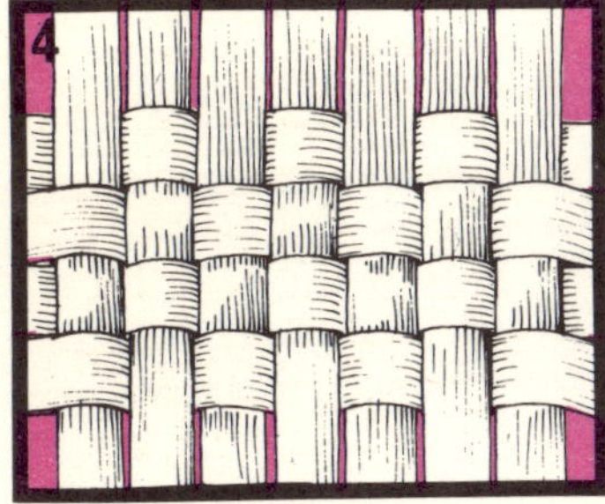

Lift first rushes again; insert another rush. Repeat until you have used all 18 in. rushes. Push them close together.

Check the measurement. It will depend on thickness of rushes. Weave more 18 in. lengths in. until check is 12×8 in.

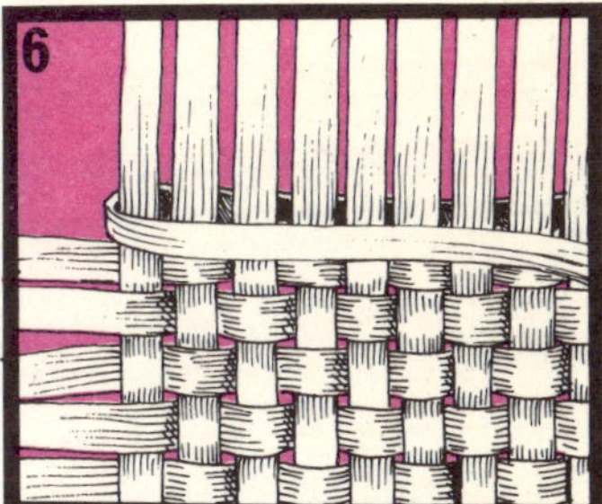

You are now ready to begin the pairing pattern. Take a long, thin piece of rush; double it. Loop round one corner spoke.

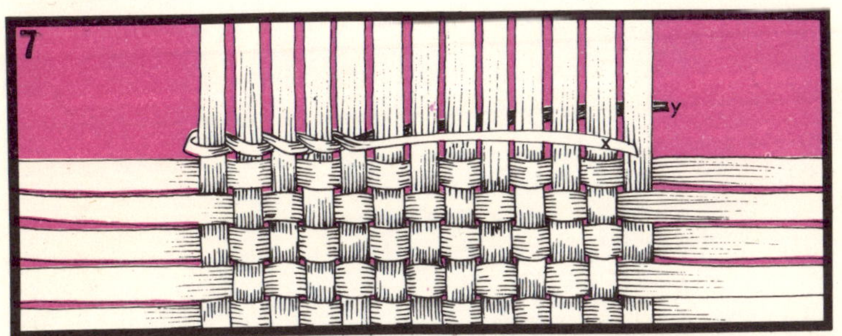

Pass(x) over(y) in front of the first spoke and behind the second spoke. Pass(y) over(x) in front of the second spoke and behind the third. Continue 'pairing' in this way, adjusting tension as you go. After one complete row, stand the mould on the base.

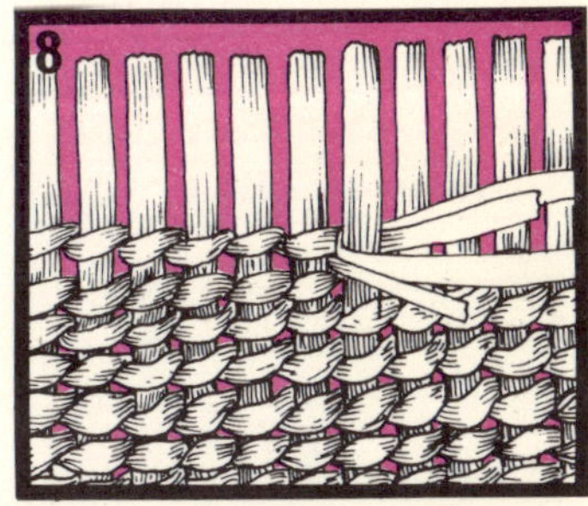

As you proceed, draw the corner spokes together until the gap is closed. Add new weavers to spoke ahead; work in together.

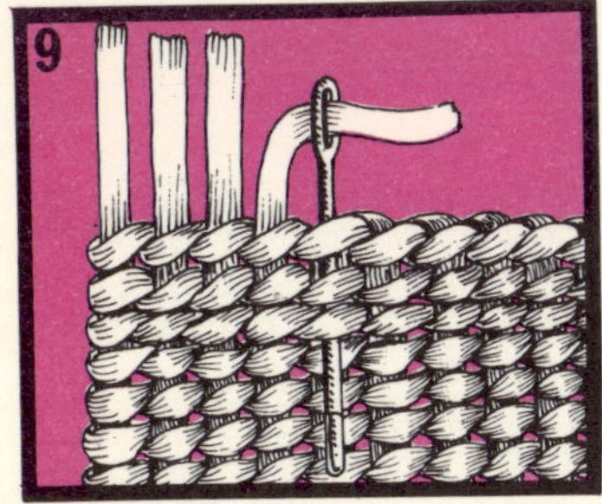

Work up sides for 2 ins. Remove mould. For border, push large needle through the four rounds; thread in the previous spoke.

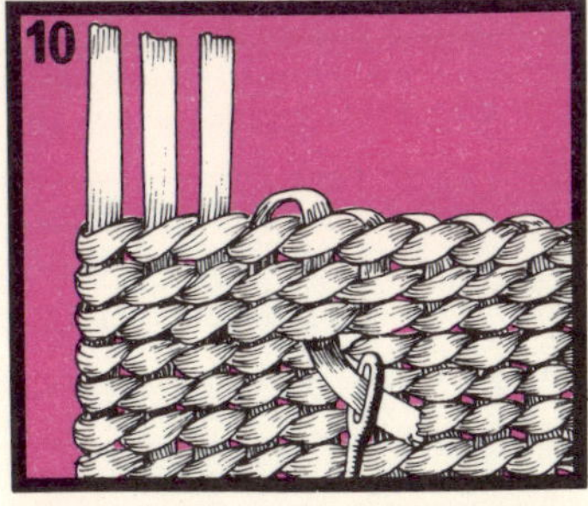

Bring needle down; trim end of rush close to the work, making a diagonal cut. Continue all round to complete border.

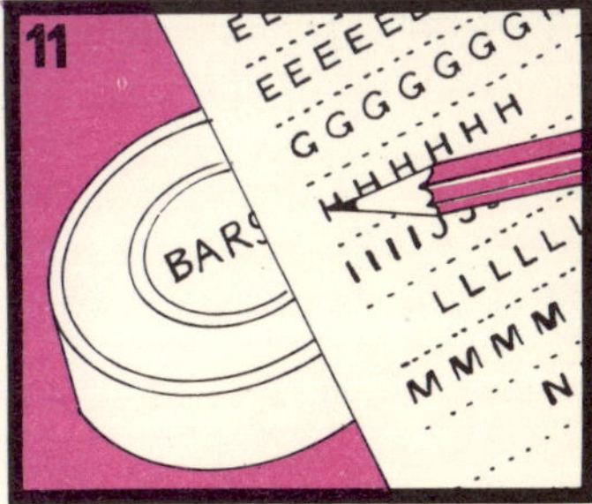

With a pencil or ball-point pen, transfer the instant lettering on to the jar caps, taking care to make the spacing even.

A Swinging Success

There's nothing quite so relaxing as gently swinging in the shade on a hot summer's day ... and you can give your friends this very pleasure—with a macrame hammock. Easier to make than it looks, it involves only four macrame knots and you can practise these until you can do them automatically before embarking on the project. The netting, by far the major part of the work, is done very simply with half-hitches over a spacing pole and grows like magic. The overall length of the hammock is 104 ins. Between the dowels, stretched out flat, it is 74 ins., and 24 ins., wide. Choose the yarn carefully. It is important to have one which will hold the knots without slipping. Polished yarns need washing first. Don't be alarmed when the string curls and twists. It looks as if a regiment of cats has played with it for hours, but it won't tangle and you can wind it into balls when it is dry.

YOU WILL NEED:
6 1 lb. balls of heaviest polished parcel twine (or piping cord, but this is more expensive)
1 6 ft. length of 1 in. dowelling
Saw · sandpaper · ruler
Wax or polyurethane varnish
36 in. length of ½ in. dowelling for spacer rod
Piece of soft wallboard 24 ins. × 36 ins. for working surface
Felt-tip pen
Long pins
2 3 in. iron rings
Thick acrylic adhesive

To begin practising knots, pin a cord on to a piece of board. Cut 18 in. lengths; double them mount with Lark's Head knots.

To work Horizontal Double Half-Hitch (which in the hammock is to be worked over dowel) pin right-hand cord across the others (a). Bring next cord over, behind and through loop (b). Tighten. Then over, behind and through loop again (c). Continue along row.

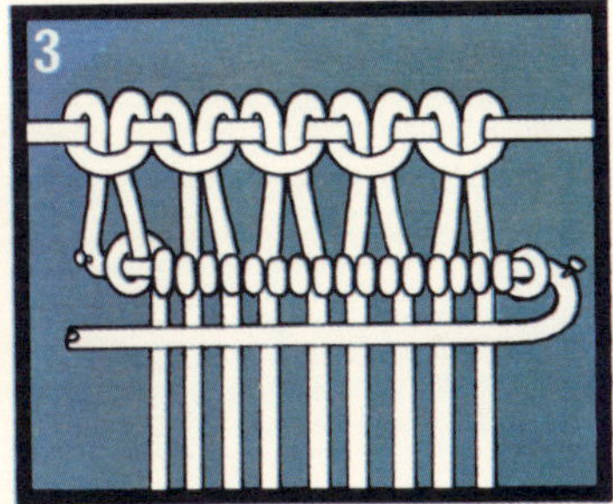

A completed row of Double Half-Hitch looks like cording. When you work it on the dowel, push knots together, without gaps.

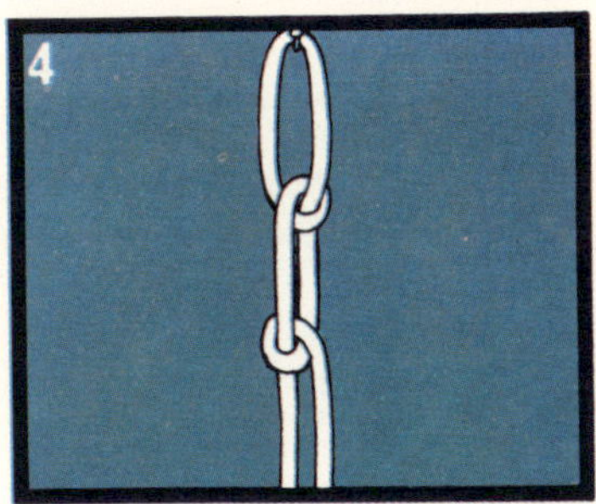

Practise Half-Hitches with one cord, doubled. Knot one end over other, under and through loop. Repeat. Tighten.

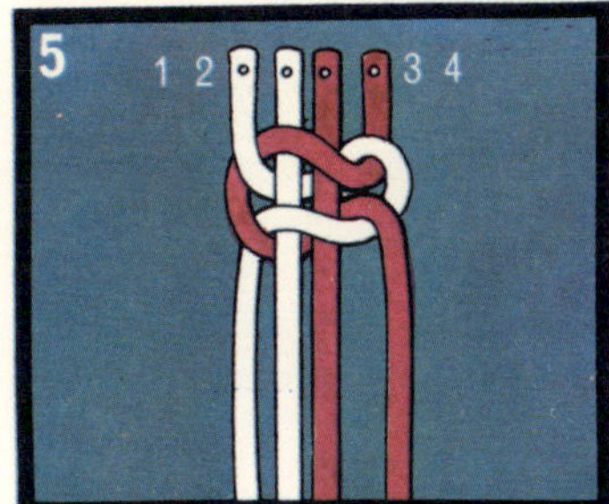

Half-Knot: mount 2 cords. Take cord 1 under 2 and 3: 4 under 1, over 3 and 2, through loop; then over 1, under 2 and 3 through loop. Tighten.

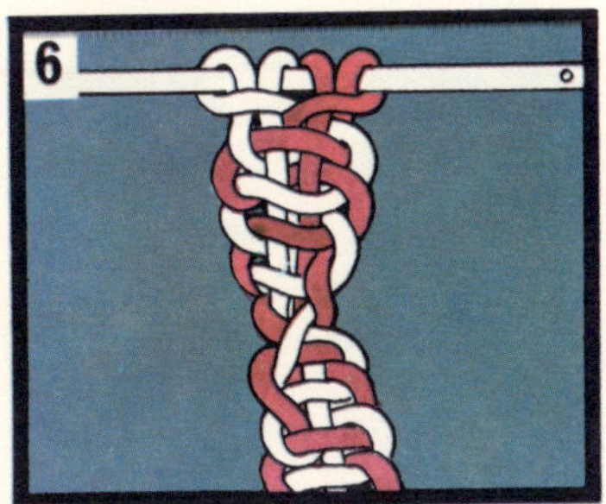

As you continue down the row, working with 1 and 4 (cords 2 and 3 are filler cords) the work will twist into a spiral.

The only other knot you need is Overhand knot. This is a loop, formed with one or more cords, often used for fringing.

To wash the string, tie in loose skeins and wash thoroughly in hot water and detergent. Dry outside and wind in balls.

Cut 44 lengths of parcel twine, each 9 yds. long. For easy working, bundle up cords and wrap ends round to secure.

Saw dowelling in half and sandpaper ends until slightly rounded and smooth. Polish with wax or clear polyurethane.

With felt-tip pen, draw parallel guidelines across the soft board at 3 in. intervals. This is the depth of each diamond.

Mount each cord $2\frac{1}{2}$ yds. from end on to dowel with Double Half-Hitches. The first example, on left, shows knot loosely tied, for clarity. In the centre, knot is tightened as it should be. On right, the reverse of the knot is shown, tightened.

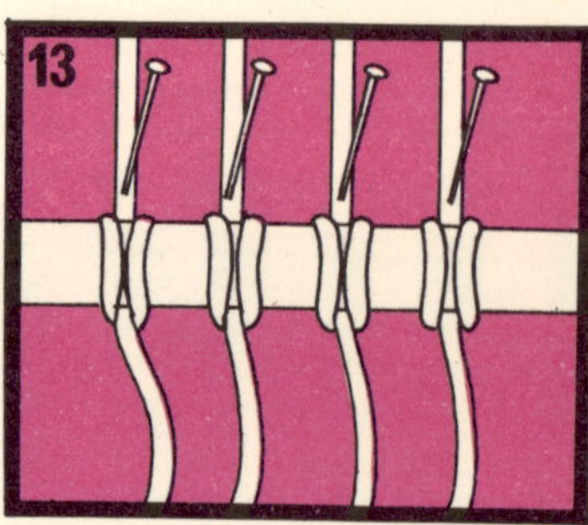

To anchor the work to the soft-board working surface, stick long pins through the cords close to the dowelling.

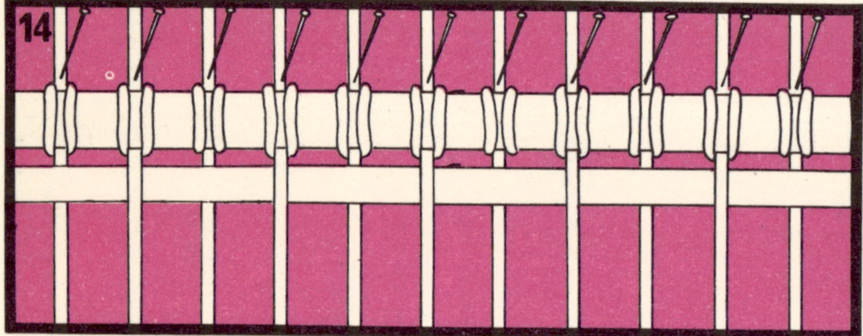

Lay the spacing rod against the dowel, weaving through knotting cords, thus: take the stick over the first 2 cords, then under and over all the other cords alternately until you come to the last 2 cords. Take the stick over these, to match beginning.

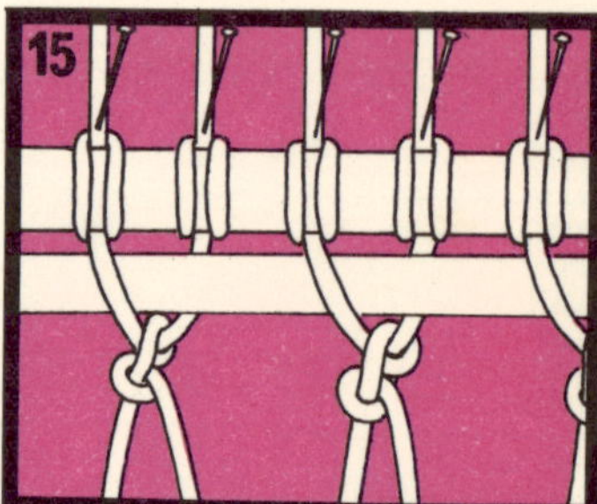

Tie 2 Half-Hitches with each 2 cords around the spacer. Make sure first HH is round one cord and second round the other.

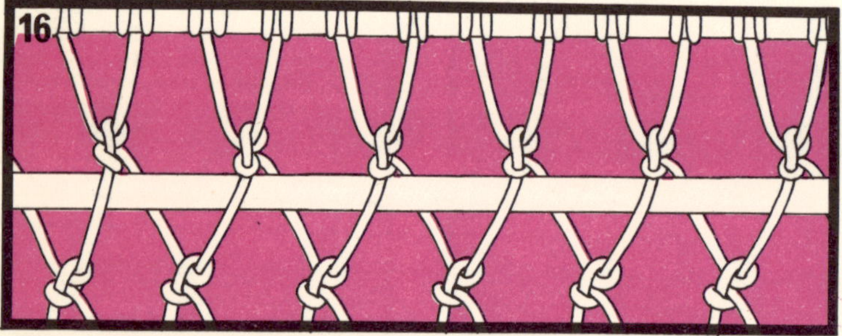

This is called the See-Saw knot or Half-Hitch chain. For second row, weave spacer through knotting cords again and tie 2 HH across row: Leave aside first (double) cord, tie with next 2 and so on. Leave aside last (double) cord. This makes netting pattern.

Continue knotting in this way until work is 74 ins. long. Check rows are level with parallel lines on the board.

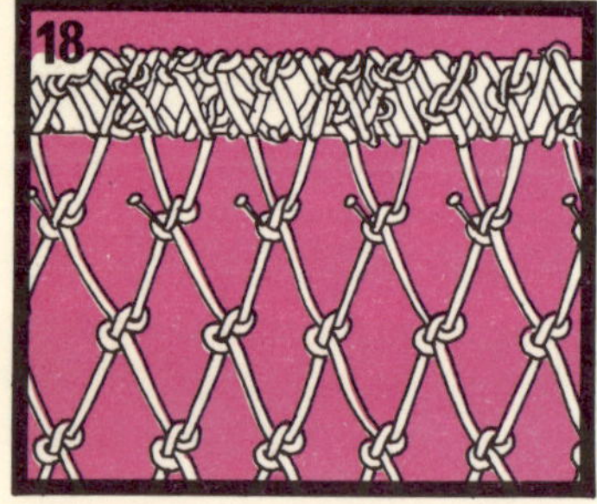

Move work up working surface as necessary, pinning it in place through knots. Keep it level across width.

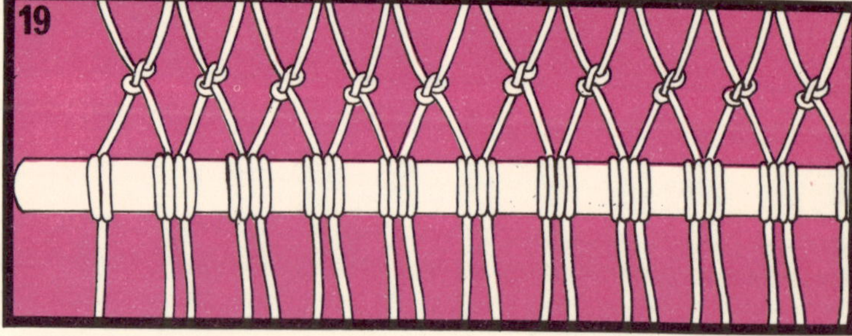

Complete the main part of the hammock by attaching the cords to the other length of polished dowel with Double Half-Hitches. The knots must be pulled tight and separated in groups of 4. Now you are ready to work the V-shaped ends of the hammock.

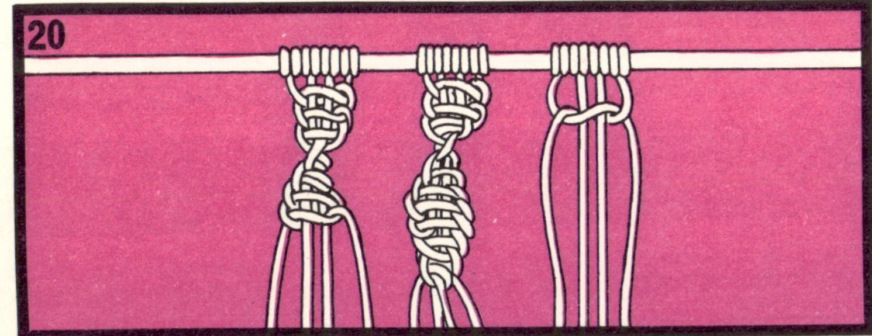

To make the spiral twists, tie 7 Half Knots with first group of 4 cords, 11 with second group, and so on to about 21 in the centre group. Decrease towards other side. You will have worked 11 spiral twists with 11 groups of 4 cords, as shown.

Take all cords through an iron ring and back down to the dowel, leaving a space of about 18 ins. between the dowel and the ring.

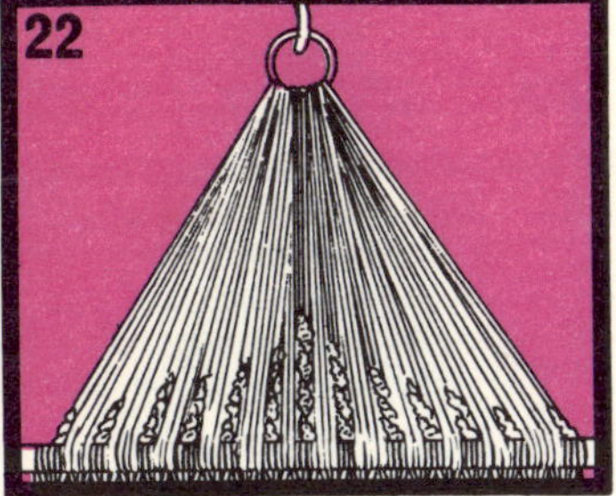

Tie each outside group of 6 cords loosely round dowel to set tension. Hang work from a hook; it will be easier to keep tension.

Start tying from one side. The first 6 cords will go in first gap between spiral twists. Tie a Double Half-Hitch with each cord.

The next 4 cords are tied in the next gap, and so on, ending with the last 6 cords in the last gap at other end. Keep tension even.

Cut $1\frac{1}{2}$ yd. length of twine. Wrap cords as close to ring as possible: with ring on right, lay a long loop over cords, leave a long end to pull. Wind tightly from left to right towards ring 10 times. Make sure that loop still shows at right-hand side.

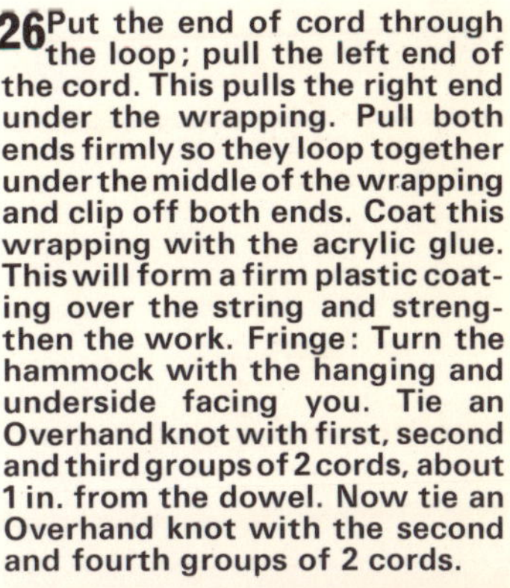

26 Put the end of cord through the loop; pull the left end of the cord. This pulls the right end under the wrapping. Pull both ends firmly so they loop together under the middle of the wrapping and clip off both ends. Coat this wrapping with the acrylic glue. This will form a firm plastic coating over the string and strengthen the work. Fringe: Turn the hammock with the hanging and underside facing you. Tie an Overhand knot with first, second and third groups of 2 cords, about 1 in. from the dowel. Now tie an Overhand knot with the second and fourth groups of 2 cords.

Continue across, tying Overhand knots with each following group of 4 cords–2 from each of above groups. Work a second row.

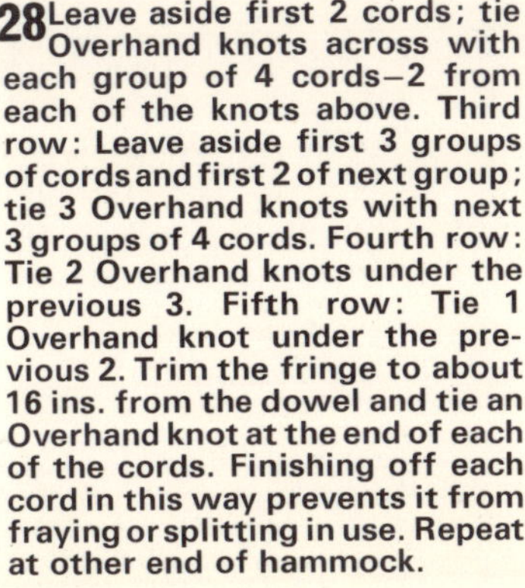

28 Leave aside first 2 cords; tie Overhand knots across with each group of 4 cords–2 from each of the knots above. Third row: Leave aside first 3 groups of cords and first 2 of next group; tie 3 Overhand knots with next 3 groups of 4 cords. Fourth row: Tie 2 Overhand knots under the previous 3. Fifth row: Tie 1 Overhand knot under the previous 2. Trim the fringe to about 16 ins. from the dowel and tie an Overhand knot at the end of each of the cords. Finishing off each cord in this way prevents it from fraying or splitting in use. Repeat at other end of hammock.

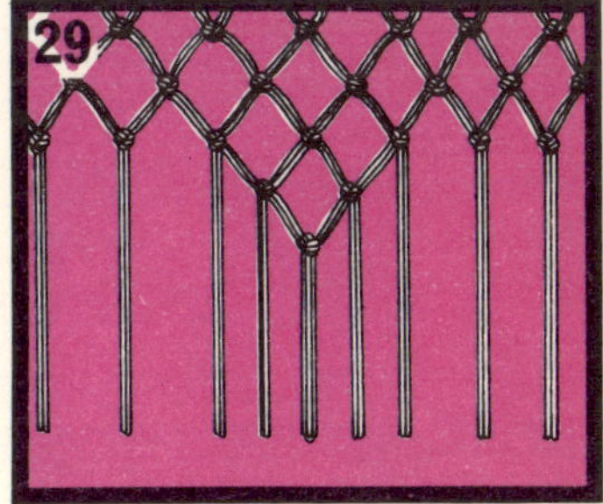

You can see in detail, above, the fringe that decorates each end of the hammock. You could, of course, make it much longer.

An Elegant Setting

The see-through look has spread to ornaments! You'll spot them in the shops—blocks of clear plastic in which decorative objects are 'trapped'. They're very elegant little items—and often very pricey! So why pay so much when you can produce them yourself at a fraction of the cost—*and* have the enjoyment and satisfaction of creating such lovely gifts. As a craft this is becoming very popular, and several brands of plastic (usually containing a base plastic and a hardener) are available. Here we suggest taking an old clock to pieces for its decorative cogs and springs, and setting them in moulds of different shapes to form a group which can be arranged in a variety of ways. Before setting, the moulds must be wiped out with special release wax to ensure the finished settings can be taken out easily.

YOU WILL NEED:
Clear-setting plastic and hardener
Plastic or pottery moulds
Mould release wax
Old clock from which to take parts
Colouring pigment if liked
Fine wet-and-dry sandpaper
Clear nail varnish
Metal cleaner

Take out cogs, springs, etc., from an old clock, choosing the most decorative ones for use. Polish them with metal cleaner.

Rub insides of moulds with mould release wax, leave a few minutes, then polish with paper tissue. Repeat this process again.

Mix a small quantity of liquid plastic with hardener in proportions recommended by the manufacturer.

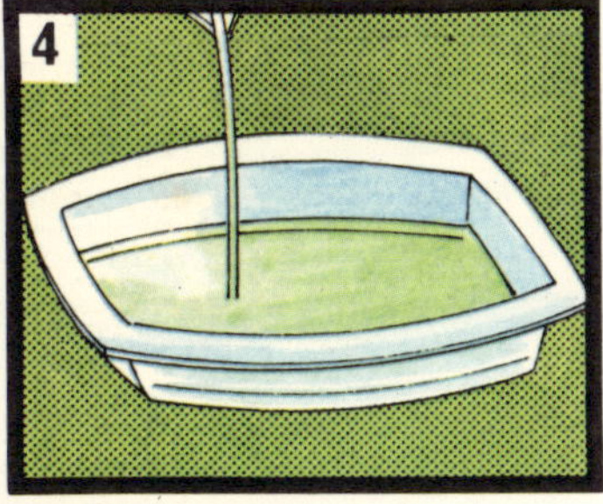

Pour a little (not more than ½ in.) into the bottom of each mould. Leave to set according to manufacturer's instructions.

Arrange first group of clock parts on plastic layer in moulds, leaving spaces in between so the second layer of parts will show. Mix a larger quantity of plastic and hardener together and pour it over clock parts to cover them completely. Leave to set.

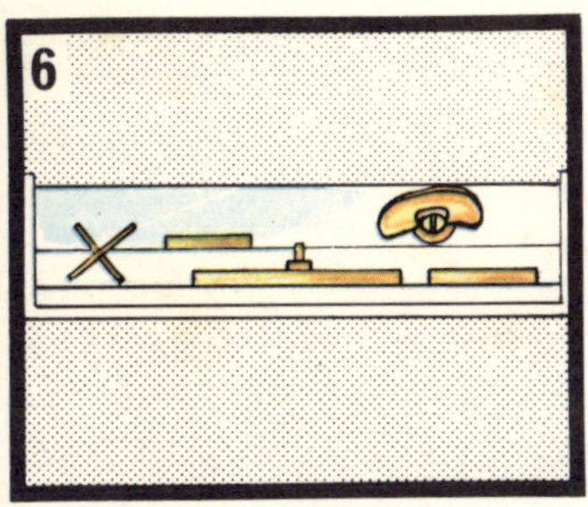

When set, arrange second layer of clock parts in the same way; mix plastic and pour over. Leave until set.

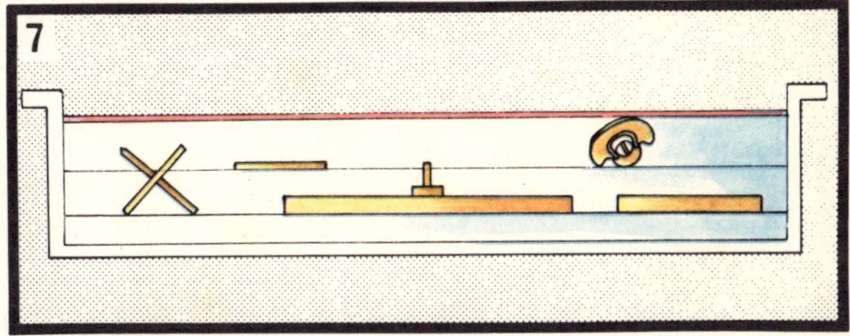

If liked, mix a final small quantity of plastic and colour with special pigment to give a coloured back layer when set.

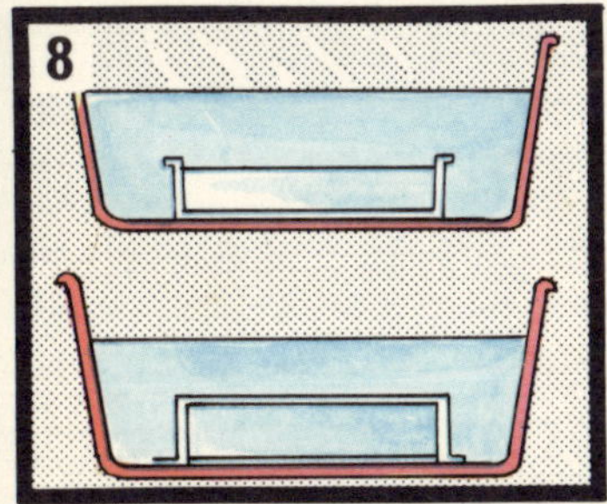

To release settings when dry, immerse for 10 minutes in hot water, then upside down in cold water for 10 minutes. Repeat.

Release settings by tapping out of moulds, lightly rub back with fine wet-and-dry sandpaper, smoothing edges.

Polish by painting with a coat of clear nail varnish or with a little clear liquid plastic mixed with hardener.

Build A Bagatelle Board!

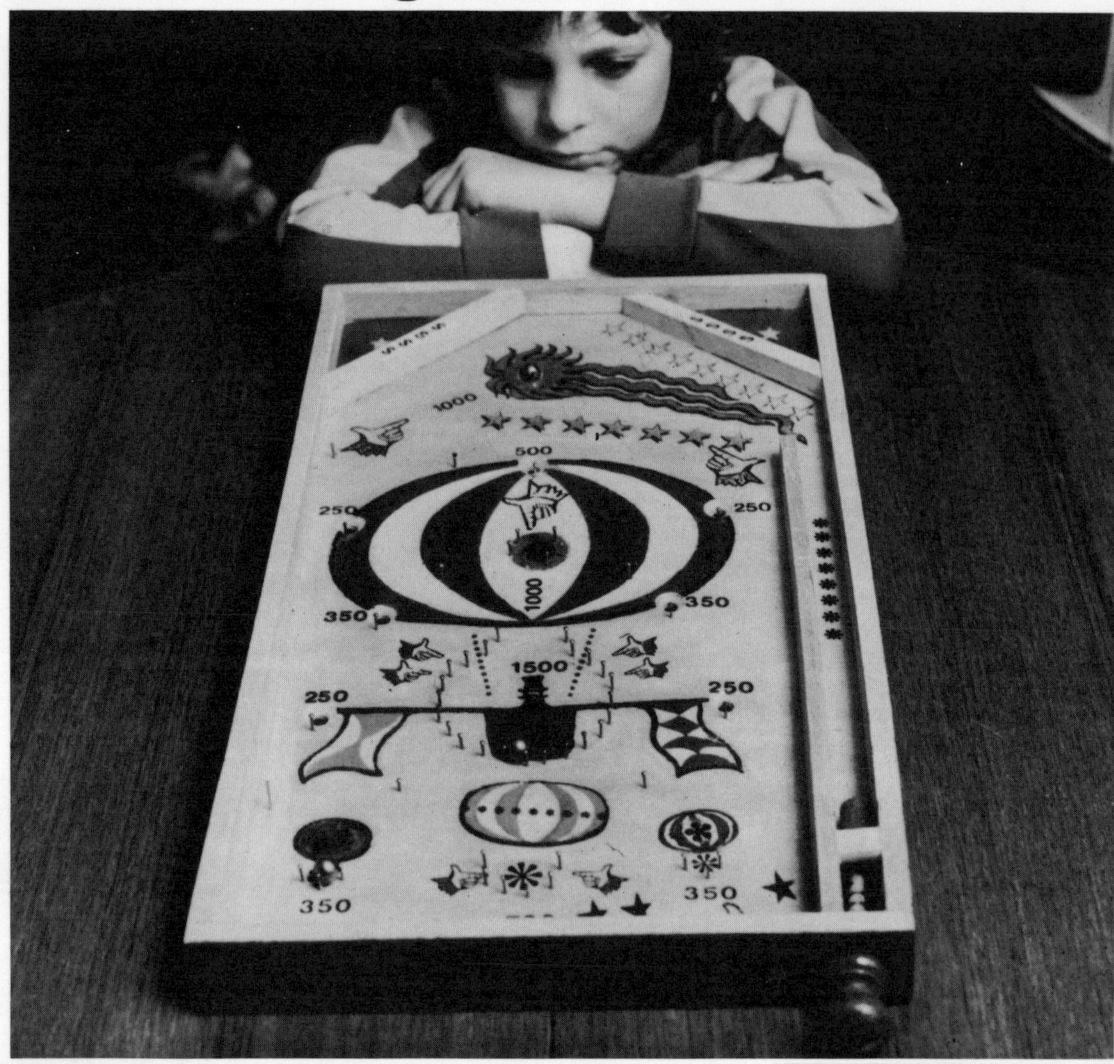

Every child—and many an adult too—enjoys playing on a bagatelle board. They are simple to make and can be gaily decorated with freehand drawings and instant transfer motifs—and there's plenty of scope for imagination! If you don't want to make the board yourself, buy the cheapest one around and cheer it up with a pop art design.

YOU WILL NEED:

Hardwood: 2 ins. by $\frac{1}{2}$ in.–
2 pieces 1 ft. 9 ins. long
2 pieces 1 ft. long
1 in. by $\frac{1}{2}$ in.–
1 piece 1 ft. 2 ins. long
$\frac{1}{2}$ in. by $\frac{1}{2}$ in.–
2 pieces 5 ins. long
$\frac{1}{4}$ in. by $\frac{1}{4}$ in.–
2 pieces 1 ft. 7 ins. long
2 pieces 11$\frac{1}{2}$ ins. long
Dowel: $\frac{1}{2}$ in. diameter–
1 piece 1$\frac{1}{2}$ ins. long
$\frac{1}{4}$ in. diameter–
1 piece 3$\frac{1}{2}$ ins. long
$\frac{3}{4}$ in. screws · $\frac{3}{4}$ in. panel pins · $\frac{3}{4}$ in. scutcheon pins (small round-headed)
1 in. steel coil spring, $\frac{3}{8}$ in. diameter · Wood glue
8 steel ball bearings, $\frac{1}{2}$ in. diameter · Transfer decorations and numerals · varnish · model maker's paints

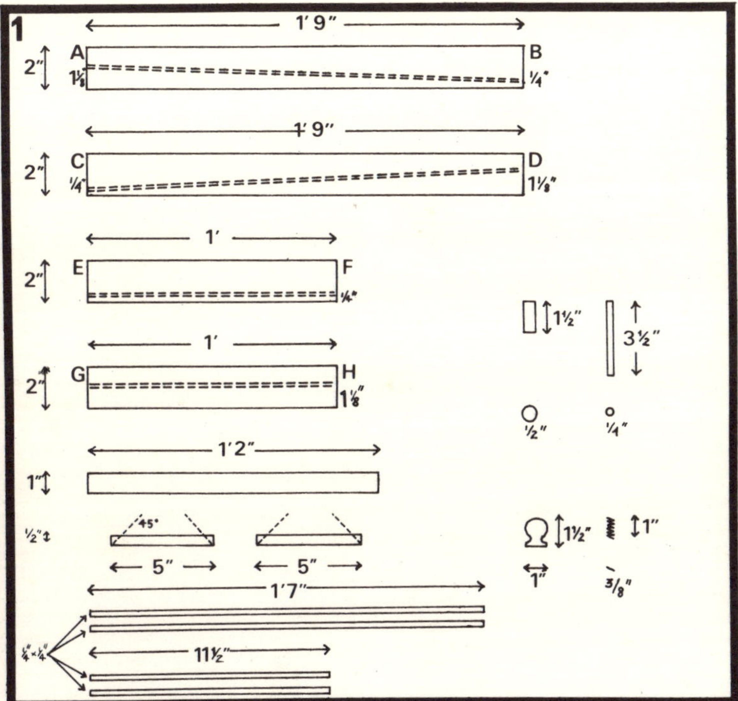

Assemble together pieces of wood and dowel etc. for board as shown, cutting off corner guides as directed and marking lines ¼ in. apart from (a) to (b), (c) to (d), (e) to (f) and (g) to (h). These lines are for beading to hold board at correct angle.

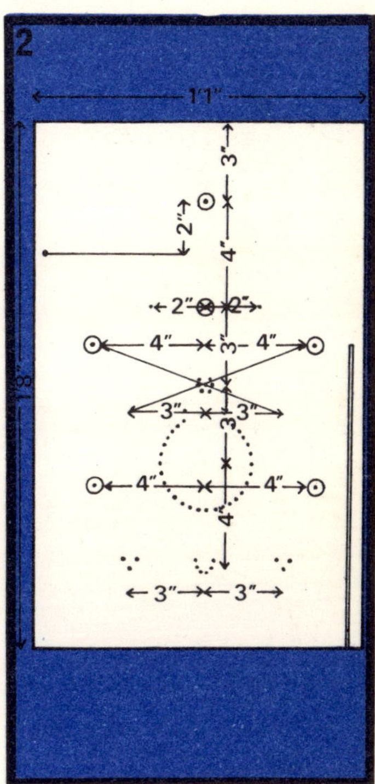

Copy pin table plan full size; place over board. Pierce nail holes with bradawl; make ball holes with ½ in. countersink.

Decorate with design as shown or to choice, using transfer motifs and painted designs. Varnish. Put in nails.

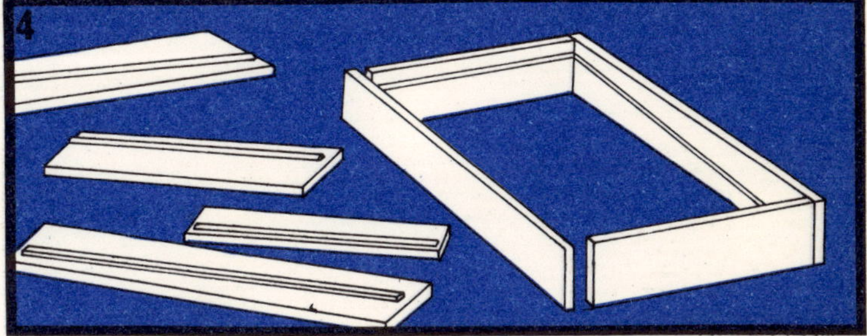

Glue and panel pin beading to frame sides along lines marked, leaving ½ in. clearance each end. Treat ends similarly, allowing ¼ in. clearance. Assemble frame, making sure (a) and (d) are at the same end, using screws and glue at corners.

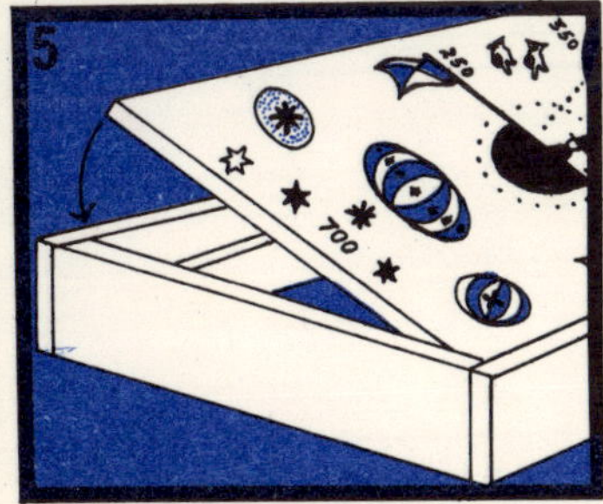

Glue round upper edge of ¼ in. beading. Drop in pin board and stand weights on until the glue sets.

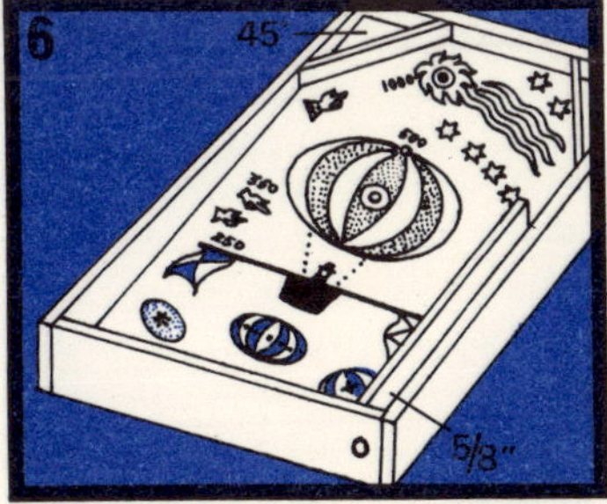

Glue in ball guides as shown. Drill hole for cue shaft ¾ in. up from bottom, 13/16 in. in from right.

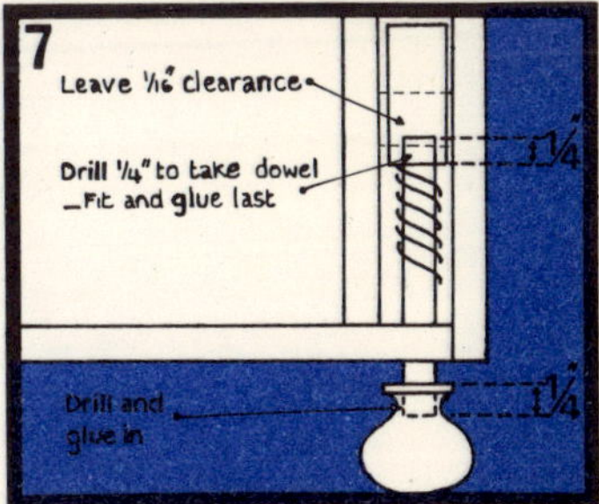

Drill, fit and glue spring cue as shown. Glue in small block of wood to prevent cue head rising.

Flowers Forever!

Give lasting pleasure to a flat-dwelling friend by taking a gift that captures all the colour and beauty of a country garden! You can dry and preserve flowers and leaves throughout the year until you have a collection that is a blend of every mood and every season. In spring you can dry daffodils, grape hyacinth, narcissus and other colourful bulbs in a granular compound. In summer you can dry some blossoms by the same method, and others simply by hanging them upside down; grasses can be hung in bunches or dried flat on trays. Leaves preserved in glycerine in early summer take on a new depth of colour and an attractive sheen, and in autumn berries and berry fruits can be preserved on the stem. Even in winter you can cut and preserve specimens—such as privet, cupressus, bay and other evergreen leaves.

YOU WILL NEED:
Drying compound such as household borax, or silica gel crystals
Glycerine or motor car anti-freeze solution · Water
Airtight container
Old vases, pots or jugs
Scissors · string · Hooks in ceiling or wall (for hanging flower bunches)
Old trays or box lids
newspapers
Selection of leaves, flowers, berries and grasses
For the arrangement shown above:
Preserved natural materials
Basket with handle
Dry holding material such as Oasis
Non-hardening modelling clay such as Plasticine

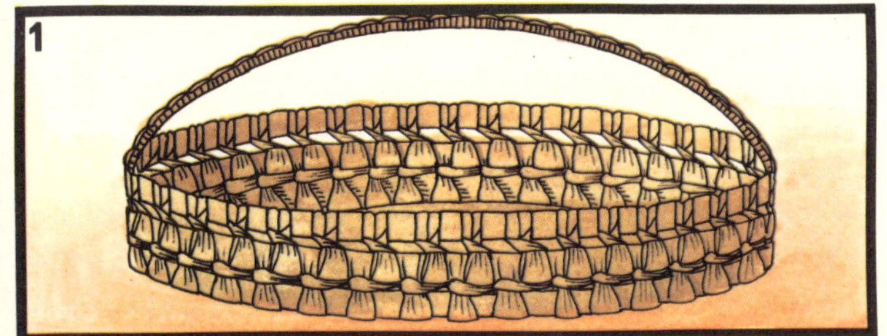

Choose a long, shallow basket with handle. It must be firm. Pack with a block of dry holding material such as Oasis.

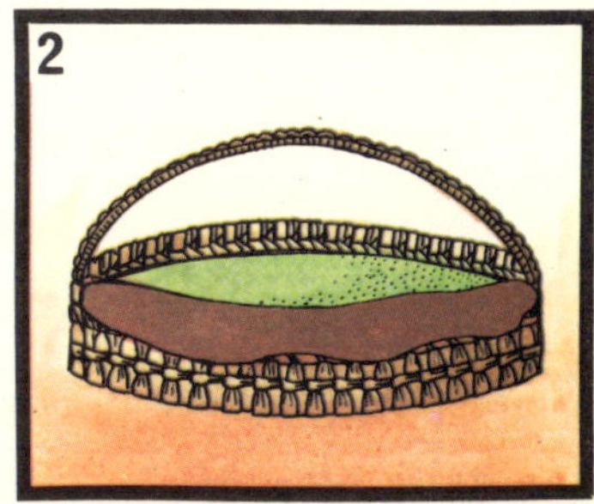

Press a thick strip of Plasticine over the front rim of the basket. This helps to hold small, low flowers.

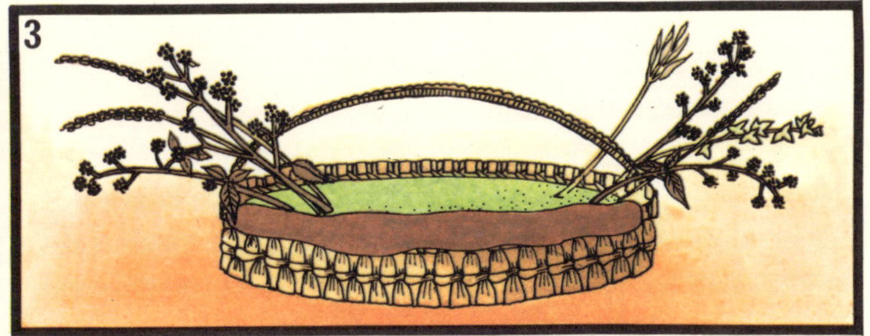

Outline the crescent shape with the longest material, e.g. preserved blackberry and ivy, dried plantain, lupin seed pods.

Place the central feature. Here it is a snipped-off head or dried giant hogweed with dried achillea heads at each side.

Keeping the crescent shape, place bright yellow dried helichrysum flowers and buds, some spilling over front of basket.

Snip off tiny sprays of preserved leaves: 2 or 3 bay leaves, beech leaves with masts, oak and cupressus.

Press into holding material between flowers (take care to cover 'mechanics'). Add sprays of dried seedheads (e.g. rue).

Add flat fan shapes of cupressus at back of design, snipping it into soft, curving shapes. Leave handle visible.

If any of the material appears too crowded, snip off unwanted or straggly leaves. Check that you have a good balance of round and flat shapes, smooth and shiny textures, and hard and soft outlines.

To dry flowers in a desiccant, cut before fully open, on a dry day. Rosebuds, Zinnias, and forsythia do well.

Cut the stems to about 2 ins. long and strip off any leaves. Pick off any damaged petals or fading blossoms before treating.

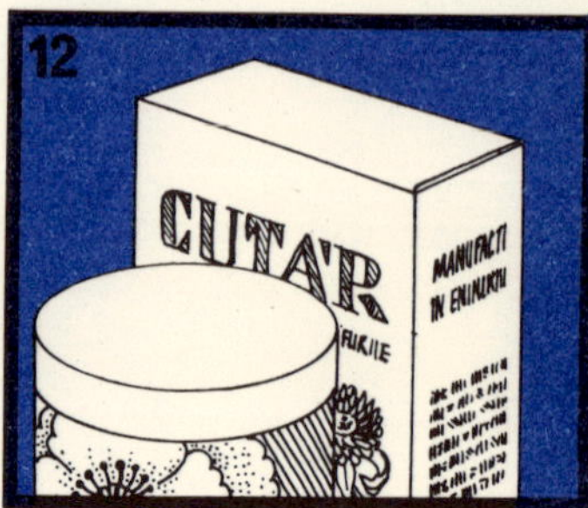

You can use household borax, or ground silica gel crystals to dry flowers.

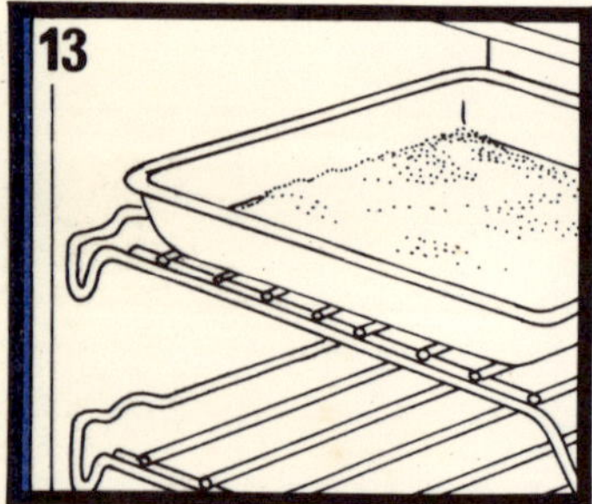

Make sure dessicant is dry. The granules turn from blue to pink as they absorb moisture. Spread on baking tray; dry in low oven.

Choose an airtight container, e.g. old cake tin, polythene, cardboard or wooden box with tightly fitting lid.

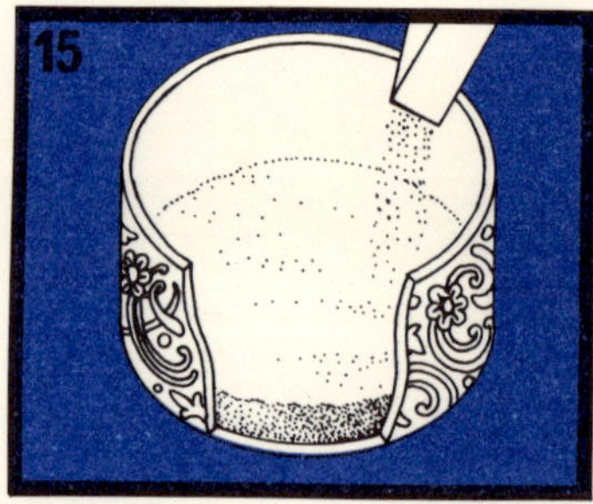

Allow about 1 lb. of desiccant for a box about 8 ins. sq. and 4 ins. deep. Sprinkle to 1 in. deep over bottom of box.

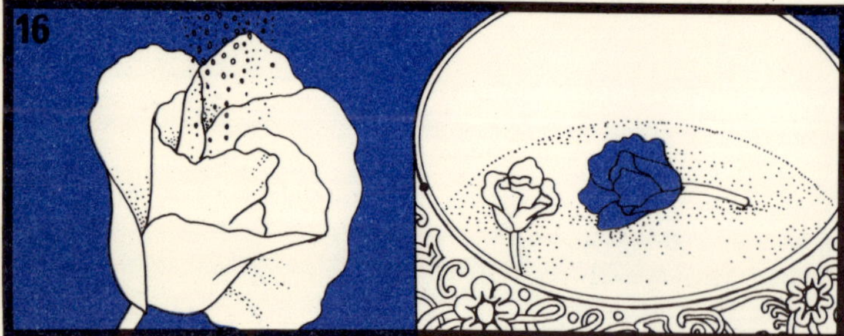

Shake the desiccant well into each flower between the petals. Carefully lay it on top of the compound in the box. Repeat with other flowers of the same type, making sure they do not touch. Cover with more compound and leave for 2–7 days.

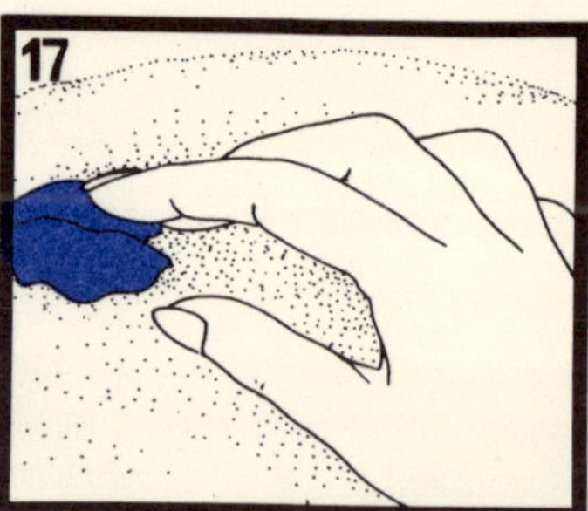

Carefully scrape away compound to check that flowers are dry. They should feel crisp but retain shape and colour.

Lay delicate grasses (e.g. Hare's tail and quaking grasses) flat on box lids or newspaper and dry in a warm, airy room.

Hang seedheads such as love-in-a-mist, rue and mallow and all everlasting flowers in bunches upside down (from ceiling or wall).

The flat, round heads or achillea, onion heads and giant hogweed can be dried simply by standing in a container. Avoid crushing.

Stand hydrangea flower heads in a jar with $\frac{1}{2}$–1 in. of water and leave until all the liquid has been absorbed.

Preserve leaves and sprays of berries in one part glycerine to two parts water, or equal quantities of water and motor car anti-freeze solution. Bring to boil; mix well. Stand plants in 2 ins. solution; leave until supple and glistening.

Absorption rate varies with thickness of plant material. Oak leaves take 1 week, laurel and camellia–4, aspidistra–13.

Heavy-tissue leaves like fig and ivy can be immersed in the warm solution. Pour into a container; press leaves in until covered.

If tips of leaves become brittle in the process, rub the leaves on both sides with cotton wool soaked in the solution.

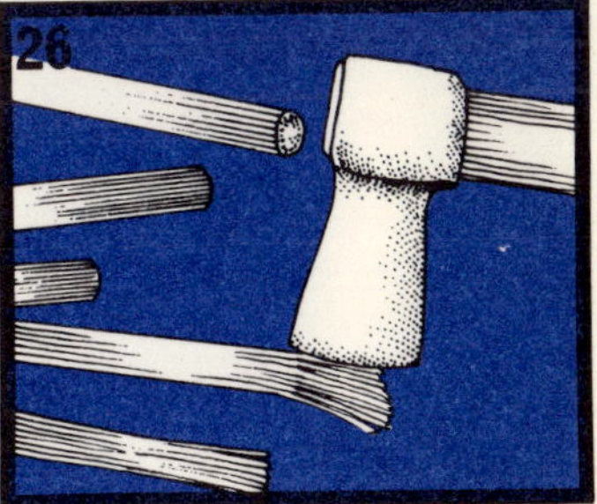

Pick evergreens (e.g. cupressus and firs) at any time of year. Crush all hard stems with hammer before standing in liquid.

Festive Furniture

There's something irresistibly romantic about old canal boats and barges. You can see them coming from a long way off, their brightly-painted shapes adding a glorious splash of colour to an otherwise sombre waterway scene. As they move majestically past, creating barely a ripple on a calm summer's day, you can pick out the gay decorations of flowers, leaves, birds and castles that so often adorn them—both inside and out. Don't worry, we're not going to tell you how to build your own canal boat—but you *can* capture the same colourful spirit of these craft in the decoration of a whitewood chest, and an enamel water jug—both of which make highly individual gifts for your homemakers.

YOU WILL NEED:
4-drawer whitewood chest
1 gal. enamel water jug
Humbrol enamel (gloss) paint
Brunswick Green, one 250 ml. tin
Bright red, one 125 ml. tin
Yellow, one no. 2 size tin
Black, one no. 2 size tin
Ivory, one no. 1 size tin
One 250 ml. tin white wood primer
One 1 in. paint brush and 1 medium size pointed paint brush
Turpentine substitute for cleaning brushes
Stiff card for stencil
Flexible steel rule · medium grade sandpaper
Piece of old cloth · sharp scissors · soft pencil

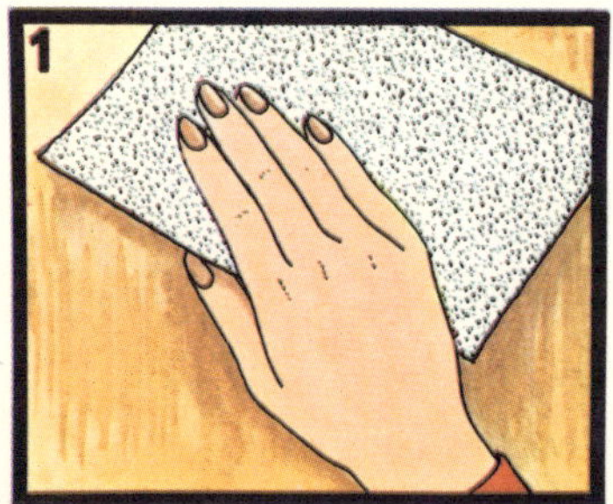

Gently rub over surfaces to be painted with medium grade sandpaper until grain is smooth. Dust with clean, soft cloth.

Paint top, front and sides of chest with white wood primer. Stand drawers on end; paint fronts. Clean brush in turps.

When priming coat is dry, sand down all painted surfaces: paint raises the grain so it must be smoothed off. Dust.

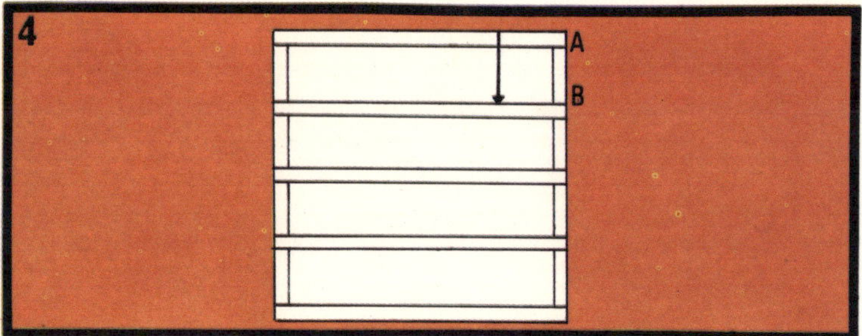

To paint yellow stripes accurately on front and sides of chest, measure from top to base of first drawer. Measure this distance down at 3 points on each side of chest. Draw feint pencil line across. Measure depth of bar between drawers; draw these lines.

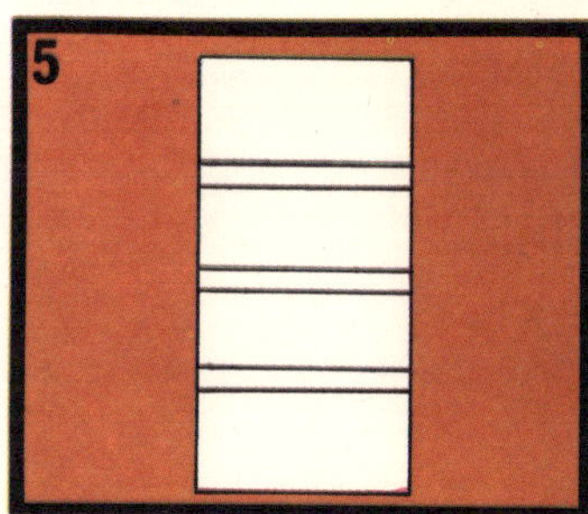

Measure the depth between the other drawers; mark the appropriate guide lines in pencil across both sides of chest.

Paint top and two drawers with green enamel. Using piece of card for straight edge, paint panels green. Cover pencil lines and leave clear channel for yellow. Leave 1 day to dry. Paint remaining drawers.

When dry, sandpaper and dust all surfaces. Give second coat of paint just as the first, allowing each colour to dry.
Paint jug (except handle) red.

Clean brushes in turps. Using card as straight edge, paint in yellow strips on the front and sides of chest with a narrow paint brush.

Using greaseproof paper and pencil, trace outlines of flowers, butterfly and leaf. Transfer outlines on to card.

For each stencil, cut a piece of card 1 in. beyond each outline. Using scissors, cut away inside portion of each shape.

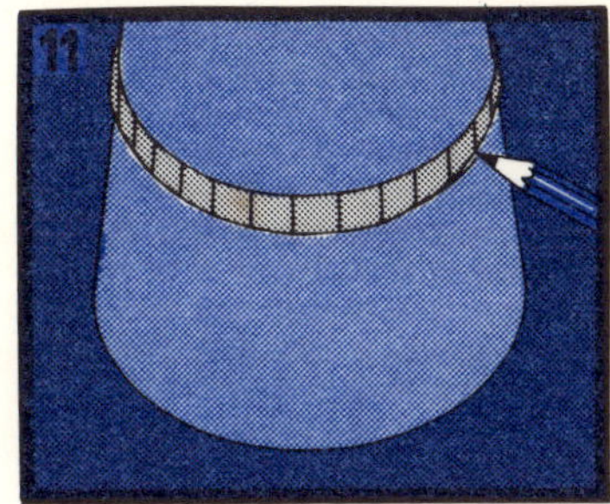

Measure 4 ins. up from base of jug. Use a flexible steel rule and draw a pencil line round jug. Draw another $2\frac{1}{4}$ ins. higher.

With ivory paint and pointed paintbrush, paint in ring of daisies between lines round jug; paint butterflies. Leave to dry.

Stencil in the larger flowers, leaves and butterflies on the drawers and sides of chest. Draw and paint as many as you like—the more there are, the gayer and brighter it will be.

When quite dry, paint handle and rings round jug. Outline flowers, leaves and butterflies on jug and chest of drawers with fine black lines. Paint in spots, veins and antennae.

Mosaic Chess Table

A super wedding present for a young couple is this coffee table with a built in raised chess board. You could make the table merely by buying a piece of plywood and four screw-on table legs which are available from do-it-yourself shops or hardware stores, or you could use an older coffee table, stripping it and painting it so it looks new or shiny. If you wanted it to be a very special present you could of course buy a new, plain wood coffee table—let yourself be guided by economics when making the choice! The chess board is worked using mosaic tiles and we suggest using $\frac{3}{4}$ in. square ones which are made in France and Italy and are probably the easiest to obtain from craft shops. To work a chess board 12 in. square you will need 128 tiles in each colour.

YOU WILL NEED:
Old or new coffee table or piece of plywood approx. 2 ft. 6 in. square
4 screw on legs (if using plywood top)
2 sheets of 1 ft. square $\frac{3}{4}$ in. glass mosaic tiles in black and white
Pencil, sandpaper, rag
Impact adhesive, grout powder
Old saucer and knife
Paint, woodstain or polyurethane varnish

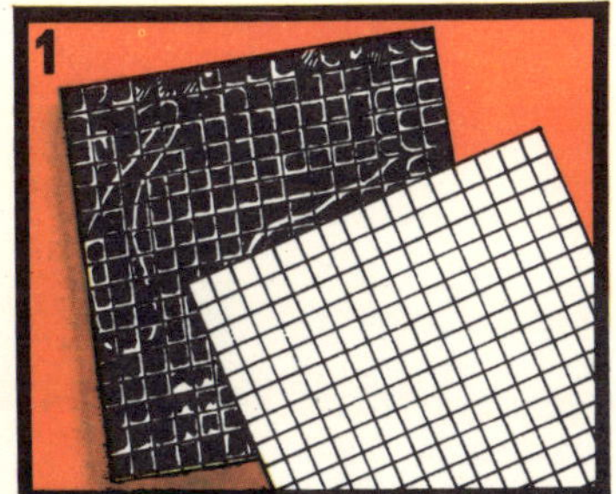

Glass mosaic tiles are bought stuck to a sheet of paper, usually 1 ft. square. Each colour is separate.

Mark a square in pencil in the centre of the table 12×12 in. Sandpaper to give a rough surface; brush off with soft cloth.

Divide each side of square into 8 equal parts. Join with pencil lines, so whole square is divided into 64 $1\frac{1}{2}$ in. squares.

Following manufacturer's instructions, spread adhesive over square on coffee table. Peel off several mosaic tiles in both colours.

Fill in each small square on your table in alternate coloured tiles. Leave a minute space between tiles for the grout.

Following directions mix grout to a smooth creamy paste in an old saucer (it should be consistency of cake icing).

Spread grout over tiles with old knife filling in all spaces. Wash off excess with a damp cloth, so tiles are fairly clean.

Leave to dry overnight. Clean again so each tile is quite free from grout. Use a nail brush to gently scrub them if necessary and make sure the outside edge of tiled square is clean and free from all grout and adhesive.

Paint outside 'frame' and legs of coffee table with wood stain, paint or clear polyurethane.

Alternatively you could work a mosaic design on the coffee table such as the one above. You will have to 'square up' all curves in the design, so draw out on graph paper first and use this as a chart to help you.

Wire Lyre

This delicate lyre bird, made very simply from wire, looks dramatic displayed against a plain background with a light source to project its shadow. If you have difficulty in buying wire which is sufficiently easy to work, yet not too thin to hold its shape, green plastic-covered garden wire is very suitable, and it can be sprayed silver or any other colour you wish when the model is complete. Fix it down to a wooden block, using small netting staples to make it stand firm.

YOU WILL NEED:
20 yds. soft wire (copper or chrome finish, or plastic-covered garden wire) about 1/16 in. in diameter.
Metallic or coloured spray paint to finish (if liked)
Small block of wood, painted black
A few netting staples
Old, strong scissors or wire cutters
Small pliers

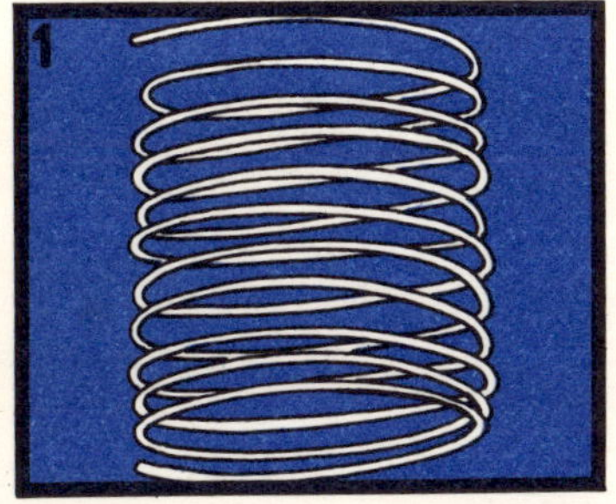

Cut off 8 yds. of wire and bend it in 2 ft. loops, as shown, to make a flat skein.

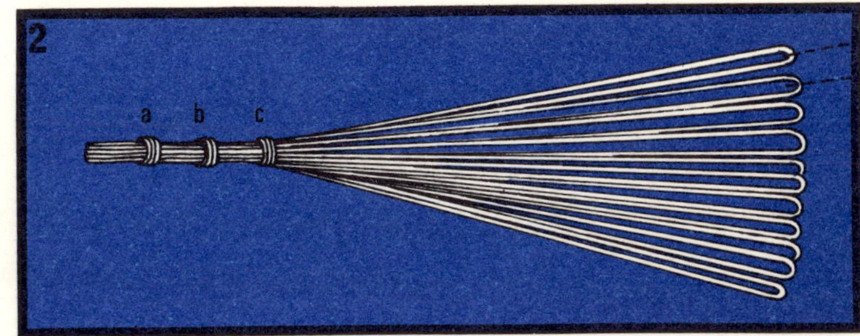

Bend the skein with more wire at (a), (b) and (c). Twist ends of binding to lock, tuck away. Cut the 11 loops at each end of skein.

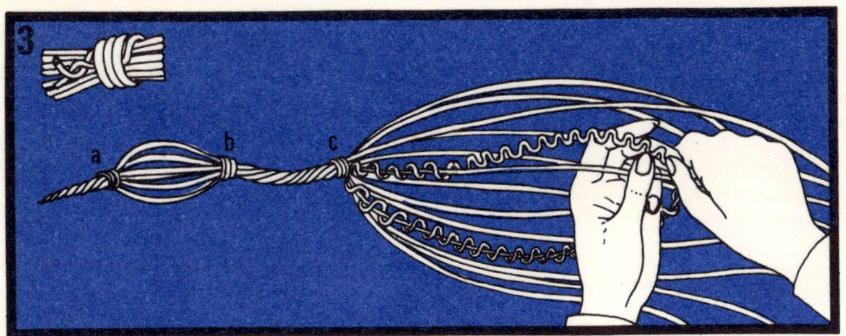

Twist short end of skein to make beak and point off with scissors. Bend each wire between (a) and (b) outward to make head, then twist neck. Bend every alternate long wire in S-shaped curves and interlace each with an adjacent straight wire.

Bind wire at (d) 4 ins. from (c). Leave $1\frac{1}{2}$ ins. free end on binding for later. Bend centre wires out to form body shape.

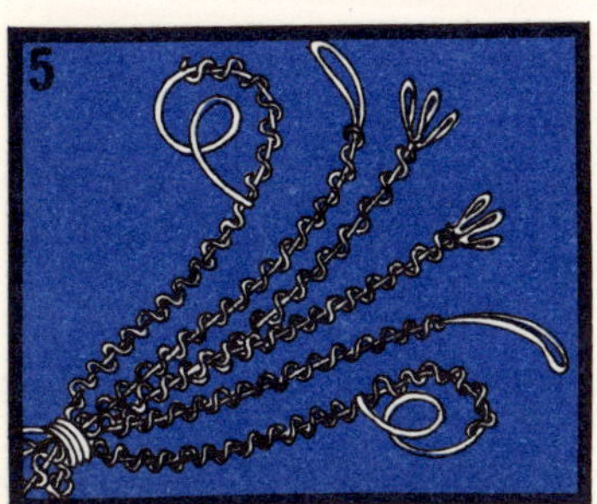

Carefully bend all tree wires in flowing curves to make lyre bird's tail, varying 'feathers' as shown in photograph.

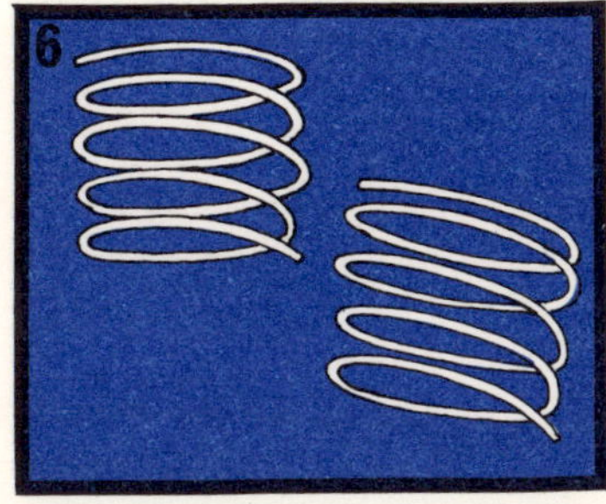

Make two 1 ft. skeins with 4 yds. of wire in each for wings and legs. Remember one wing is mirror image of other.

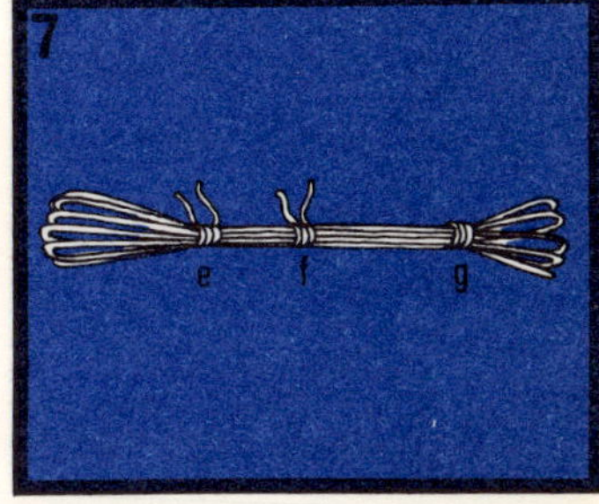

Bind at (e), (f) and (g) as shown. Loops at short end only should be cut and opened fanwise to form feet.

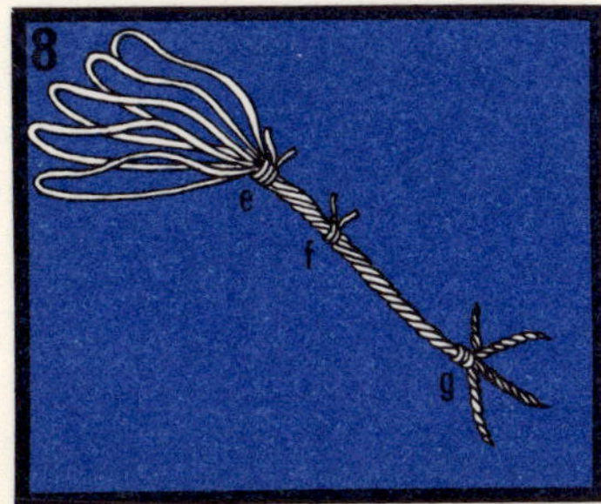

Shape loops at longer end to form wing fans. Shape between (e) and (f) to fit body. Twist toes, curves and point.

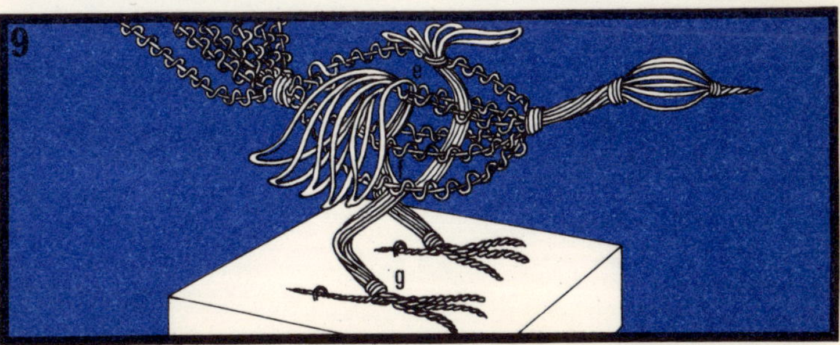

Fit wing and foot pieces in body. Bind with loose ends at (e) and (f). Bend legs and fasten toes to plinth with netting staples (g).

Pebbles For Prettiness

A set of pebble jewellery is a charming present, particularly as it is really individual. No two Baroque stones, (those which are not cut before polishing) are exactly alike, so every ring, necklace, brooch and earring you make is unique. The secret of attractive pebble jewellery is in careful making. Stones ill-matched to their mounts, too much adhesive used and the results can be messy and disastrous! This dramatic necklace, with its matching earrings and ring, is easy to make and requires no special equipment except a pair of small jewellery pliers.

YOU WILL NEED:
17 baroque pendant-shaped stones (e.g. stained crazy lace agate)
1 larger flat-sided stone for ring
Short gilt neck chain to fit round base of neck
17 gilt filigree bell caps (medium)
Pair gilt earring mounts to make drop stones
50 large and 50 medium gilt jump rings (this allows a few extra for loss or spoiling)
Epoxy resin adhesive
jewellery pliers
Cocktail stick · small foil dish

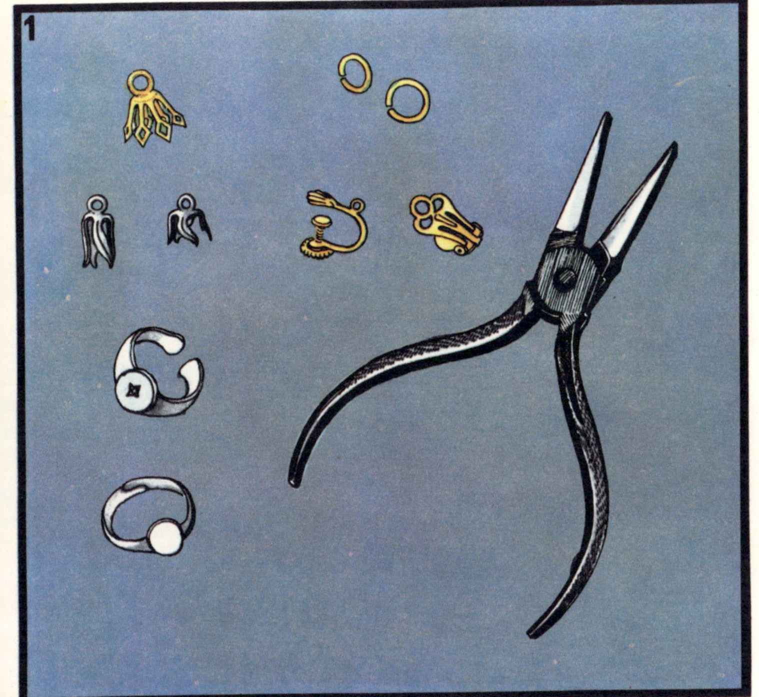

A great variety of mounts for jewellery making is available. Above shown with jewellery pliers, are some typical ones, including those used for the jewellery opposite. It is important to match the mounts and stones together, both for size and colour.

Epoxy resin adhesive is mixed as needed from 2 tubes; 'Super' type sets in 10 minutes, 'Ordinary' in 6 hours.

When setting on bell caps, stones on ring mounts, etc. place stone or mount in a small dish of salt as shown, to keep upright.

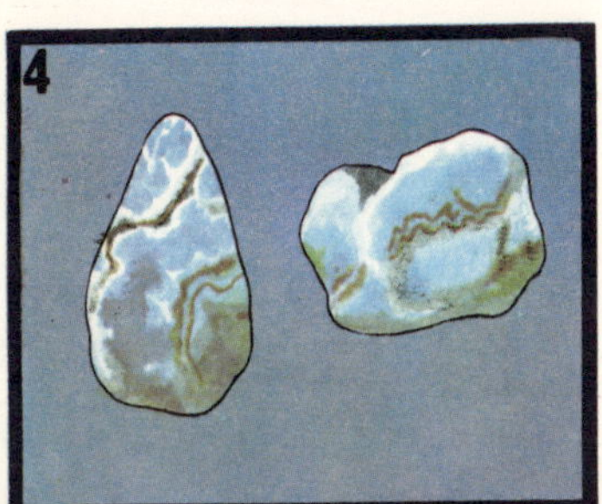

Stones for necklace and earrings must have a pointed end for bell cap. Display face of stones should have no flaws.

Choose stones of similar size for necklace, with 1 larger stone for bottom drop and 2 matched drop stones for earrings. Select a large stone for ring with a flat side for a ring mount pad and a flawless, well-marked display side.

When using quantities of small mounts, keep in separate saucers. Open jump rings with pliers before starting work.

Lay out stones with best side facing you. Press bell cap on each. Make sure 'hold' in cap faces same way as best side.

Wedge stones in salt pot, cap sitting on top, as shown. Mix adhesive and stir thoroughly with cocktail stick.

Apply a little adhesive to top of stone and to inside of cap. Wedge back in same position. Leave to set.

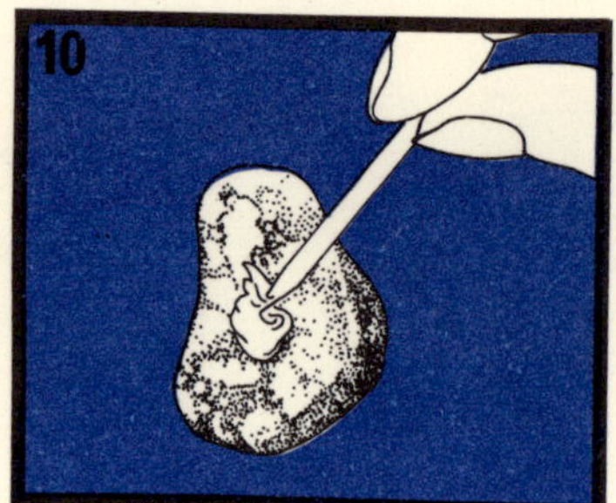

Apply adhesive to flat side of ring stone, and also to mounting pad of ring mount. Do not use too much adhesive.

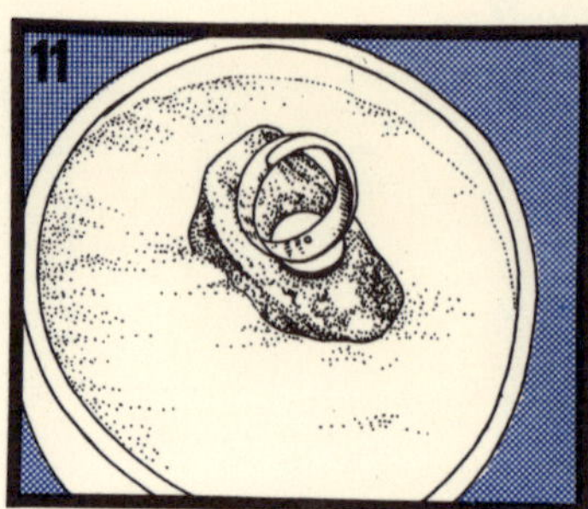

Place ring stone with adhesive uppermost in salt pot and place pad of ring mount on it as shown. Leave to set.

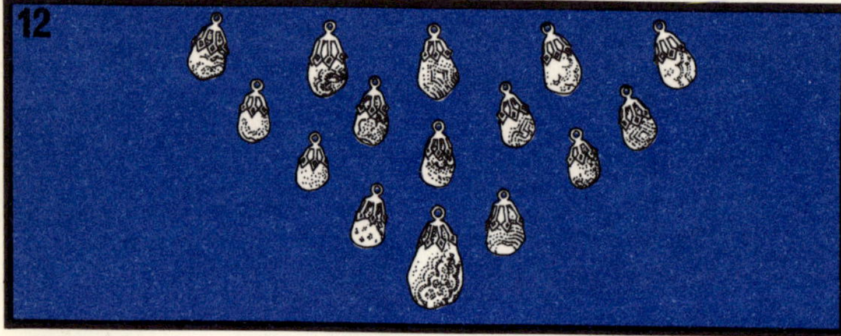

When pendant stones are completely set, lay aside the two matched earring pendants. Then lay out rest, matched as shown, on a piece of paper.

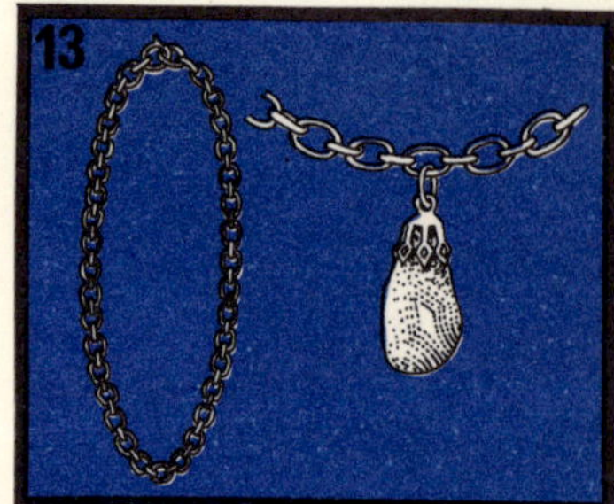

Fold neck chain to find centre. Place medium jump ring through centre link and hang pendant stone.

Lay chain flat on table, count 9 links on either side of centre pendant. On the 10th link hang another stone on a medium ring. Repeat until you have 5 stones altogether.

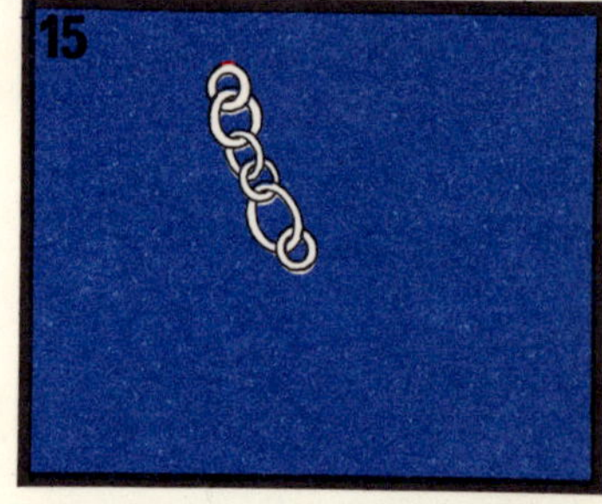

Make 4 chains of rings as shown, alternating medium, large, 2 medium, large, medium; close inner links with pliers.

On one end of each hang a stone. Attach other end to centre link of chain between fixed stones.

Make 3 chains of rings consisting of 7 medium rings and 1 large one at each end. Attach each end link through the hanging links of the 4 pendants just placed. At this stage, 9 pendant stones are in place.

Make 3 chains of 1 large, 1 small and 1 large rings. Hang a pendant stone one end of each.

Attach the other end of each chain to centre ring of linking chains, as shown. Make 2 chains, of 7 medium rings with a large one at each end. Attach end and middle links through hanging links of 3 pendants.

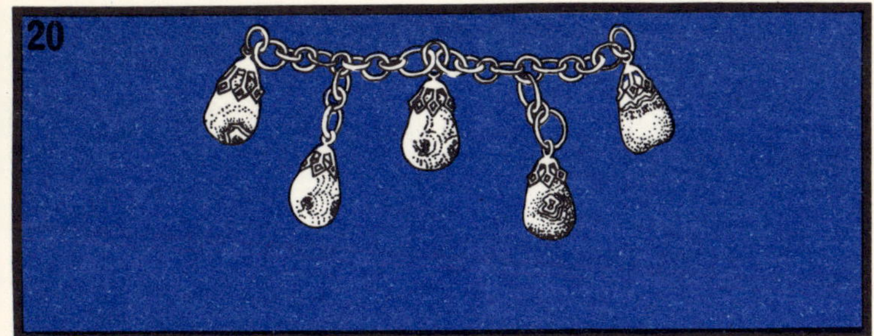

From the centre rings of these 2 chains attach 2 more pendant stones each on a large-medium-large set of linking rings.

Make one final set of linking rings–7 medium with a large one at each end–and fix between the 2 remaining pendants.

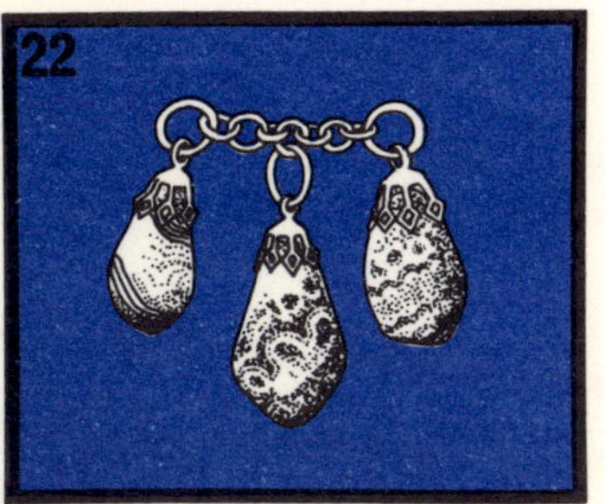

From the centre ring, hang the large drop pendant, fastening it on with a large jump ring.

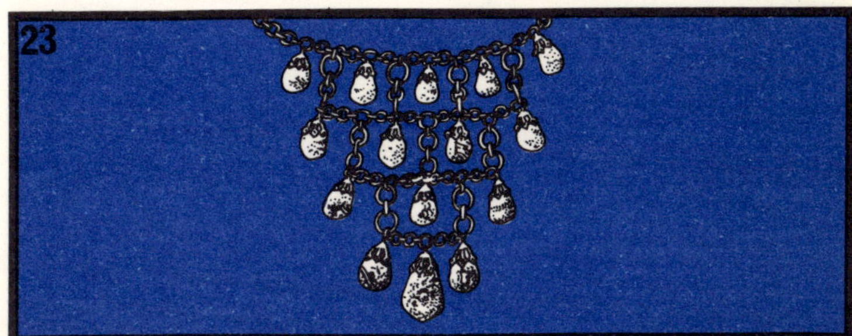

The necklace is now complete, but go over it with the pliers, tightening any rings which may not be properly squeezed together. Allow the full 'curing' time for the adhesive before wearing, according to maker's instructions.

To make the earrings, make 2 chains of 3 large rings. Attach a pendant stone on end of each chain and close.

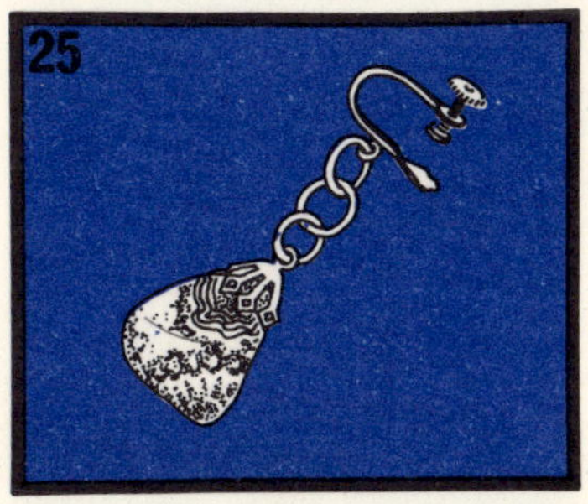

Hang other end on small ring of earring mount and squeeze each ring closed with pliers, to complete.

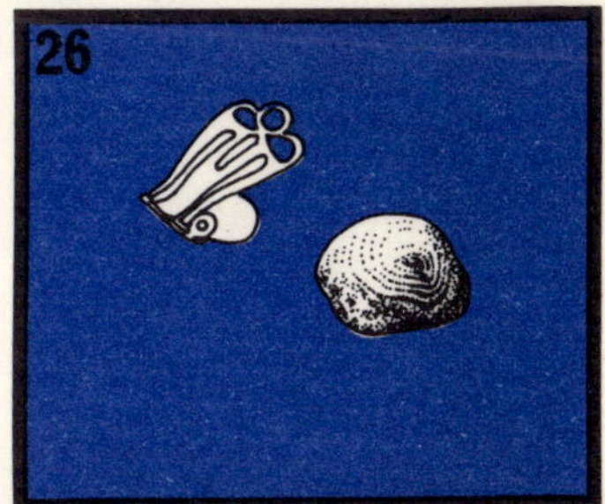

If preferred, buy flat-pad earring mounts and 2 stones, each with a flat side. This will make a pair of stud earrings.

Pot-Pourri: Fragrant Medley

To make a pot-pourri is to capture the scent of a garden. The word means 'medley', and that's just what this is—a medley of petals, flowers and leaves mixed with the spices of your choice. Dry pot-pourri can be stored in muslin, voile or net sachets, dolly bags or tiny pillows, and given to a friend to hang in her wardrobe or put among lingerie or woollens in a drawer. For moist pot-pourri, which you can keep in open bowls or in decorative jars or bottles, add salt and flower oils or essence, and keep the mixture moist with more oils. Don't leave the flowers to wither on the plant or the petals to fall. Gather them on a dry day, after the morning dew has died. You can blend the seasons in perfect harmony by drying the flowers as they blossom, and storing them in airtight containers until your collection is complete.

YOU WILL NEED:
For dry pot-pourri:
2 large handfuls of rose petals
2 large handfuls of other flowers and leaves
2 oz. ground orris root
2 oz. ground coriander
½ oz. ground cinnamon
Wide-necked jar
For moist pot-pourri:
Rose petals and other flowers and leaves as above
4 oz. common salt
½ oz. flower oil
½ oz. ground cinnamon
1 oz. each ground cloves, nutmeg, coriander
4 oz. ground orris root
Tray · weighing scales · spoon
Wide-necked covered jar

Pick the petals from the roses; spread them on a tray. Leave in a cool, dark, airy place for 4 to 5 days. Turn over daily.

Choose some flowers just for colour. Dry each type separately: try marigold and zinnia petals, larkspur, pansy, violet, mimosa.

Hang leaves to dry, then crumble. Most usual are lemon- or rose-scented geranium, thyme, mint, rosemary, sage and bay.

Dry pot-pourri: put petals and flowers in jar, add orris root (fixative) and spices. Shake well; cover; leave for 1 week.

Sew the dry pot-pourri into tiny sachets or bags made of fine fabrics. Trim with lace, ribbons and fabric flowers.

Moist pot-pourri: put dried flowers and leaves in jar. Add salt; mix well. Cover tightly. Stir daily until frothy.

Put a little orris root powder in a cup, sprinkle on the flower oil and mix thoroughly. Some chemists still sell oil of lavender, thyme, rosemary and so on. Or use cosmetic flower oil, wisteria, spring blossom or country garden fragrance.

Add fixative and flower oil mixture to jar of petals with rest of orris root powder. Stir, cover and leave 3 to 4 weeks.

Shake jar well or stir daily to distribute oils and spices. Turn out into open bowls or lidded jars or bottles.

You can add to your pot-pourri any time. Dry the plant material first and add fixative, salt and spices in right proportion.

Placing a dried rosebud on top of a bowl or jar of pot-pourri adds a pretty touch.

Pasta For Framing

The lovely decorative shapes of pasta really seem too attractive to eat sometimes—so here's a way to use them to make an unusual gift. Take a plain photograph frame, glue on pasta designs and spray it gold—and the result is a charming Victorian-style frame for a favourite portrait or photograph.

YOU WILL NEED:
Photograph frame with flat edge not less than $\frac{3}{4}$ in. wide
Selection of pasta
Rubber-based adhesive
Paint spray (suggest gold)

4 types of pasta were used—'shell', 'spiral', 'coxcomb' and 'circular'. Spiral pasta can be broken into pointed pieces.

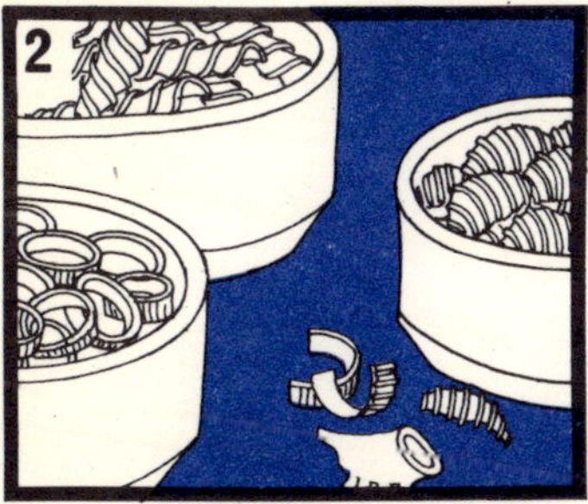

The pasta pieces should be selected, discarding any broken ones, and laid out roughly in the pattern along the frame.

Plan the top of the frame as shown, with a central motif, then lay out the two vertical sides, which should have identical patterns. The lower edge should be of a different pattern again. Adapt your design to fit the frame you are using.

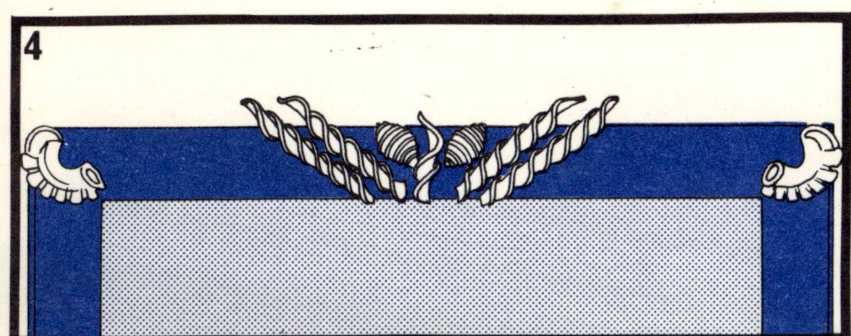

Lay the pasta to one side and work along top row first. Spread adhesive on frame and allow to set until tacky. Place two end pieces of pasta, then form the central 'fan' motif and fill in with circles. When set, stick a 'shell' open side up on centre.

Repeat the sticking along both sides, then lastly along bottom edge of frame. Allow to set thoroughly.

Take out back and glass of frame so that only edges with pasta are left, or cover glass with foil to protect it.

Spray pasta lightly with gold or other colour paint. Allow to dry, then give a second coat. Dry thoroughly; replace glass.

Owl-House Nursery Lamp

A child's lamp that makes a novel decoration in the daytime and a comforting, glowing companion at bedtime—that's the owl-house nursery lamp. If you're looking for a 'different' gift for that young niece or nephew, then this project is guaranteed to be welcomed with open arms—both by the child and its parents . . . and it's fun for you to make, too! It's built of self-hardening modelling clay—grey clay which is strengthened with nylon fibres, easy to roll out into slabs, pliable, and trouble-free in setting. For extra hardness it can be 'baked' in an oven, but this is not necessary: if preferred, you can buy a clay-hardener from your craft shop. A varnish for giving the model a gloss finish will also be useful. Lamp-holders can be bought from most chain stores—a standard fitting will transform your clay model into a practical piece of electrical equipment.

YOU WILL NEED:
Box of self-hardening modelling clay
Newspapers · $\frac{1}{4}$ in. battens
Rolling pin · sharp knife or craft knife
Paper ruled into 1 in. squares · pencil · ruler
Modelling tool or blunt-ended tool · piece of stick
Old fork · paint brush
Recommended hardener and gloss
Poster paint and emulsion paint
Piece of chipboard or plywood for base · saw
Sandpaper · screws · screw-driver · lampholder
Electric light bulb

Using several sheets of newspaper and $\frac{1}{4}$ in. battens at each side, roll out clay to even thickness of $\frac{1}{4}$ in.

Use a sharp, pointed knife or, better still, a craft knife, cut the clay with clean vertical strokes.

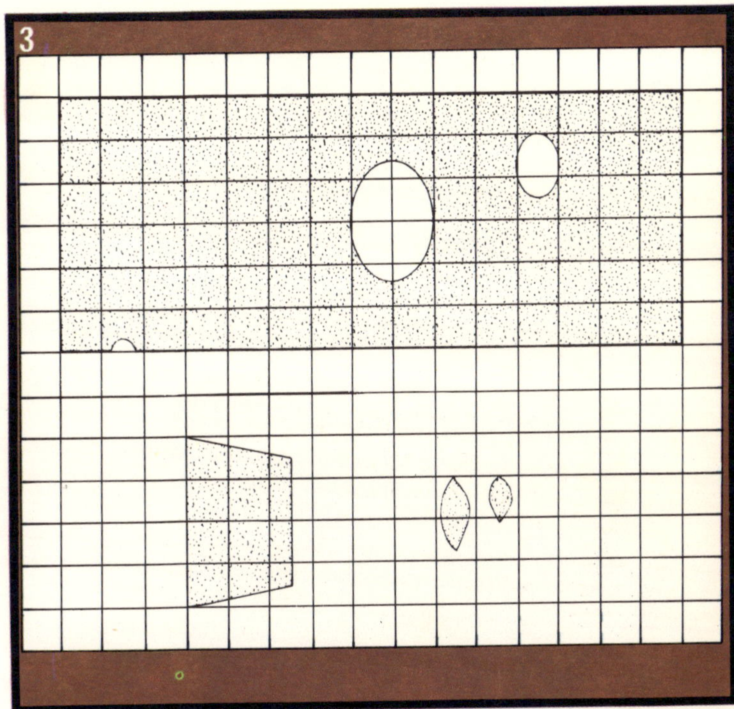

This pattern shows you how to cut out the pieces you will need for the house. Copy the shapes on to paper ruled into 1 in. squares. Cut out the main piece, 15 × 6 ins., then cut out holes where indicated, and the branch and leaf shapes.

Leave the slabs to dry for a few minutes until the clay is easy to handle. Turn pieces over once while waiting.

Tear some sheets of newspaper slightly wider than height of house (6 inches) roll them into a thick cylinder mould.

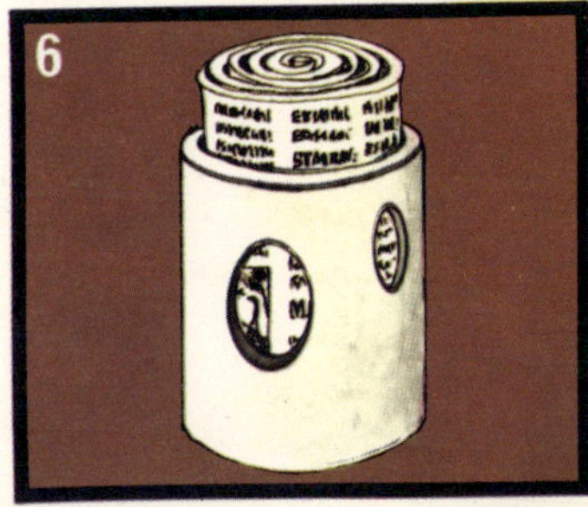

Lift the main piece of clay and wrap it round the paper cylinder so the edges meet to form a join.

Put this piece to one side and repeat with the smaller shape for the branch; wrap it round a wad of rolled-up newspapers.

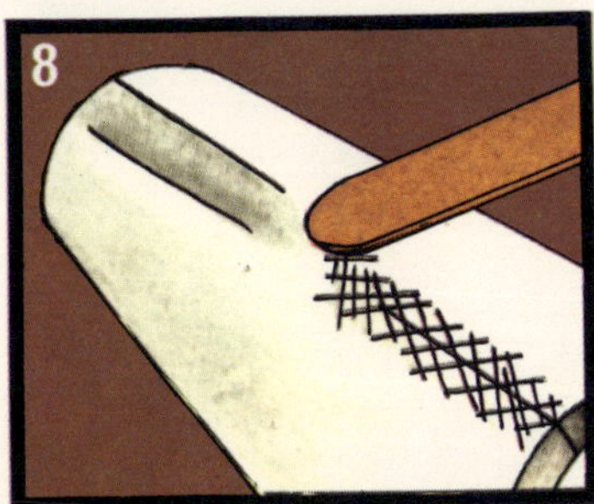

Using a blunt-ended tool, 'stitch' together the joins of the main piece and of the branch with criss-cross cuts.

Use the same stitching method on both inside and outside, joining the branch to the hole left in main piece.

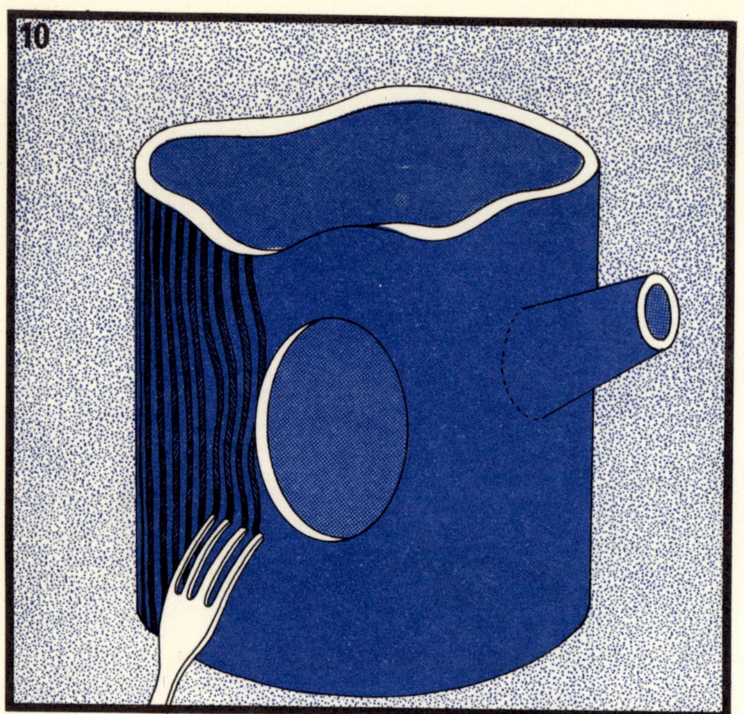

Leave main house piece to set a little. Using sharp knife, cut away, leaving wavy line round top of trunk. Using old fork, score all over outside to leave a rough surface resembling bark. Brush away loose clay.

Dampen undersides of pieces you have cut for the leaves. Press them in sprays on each side of the opening.

Using a blunt tool or piece of stick, add veins to the leaves. The main part of house is now complete; leave to dry.

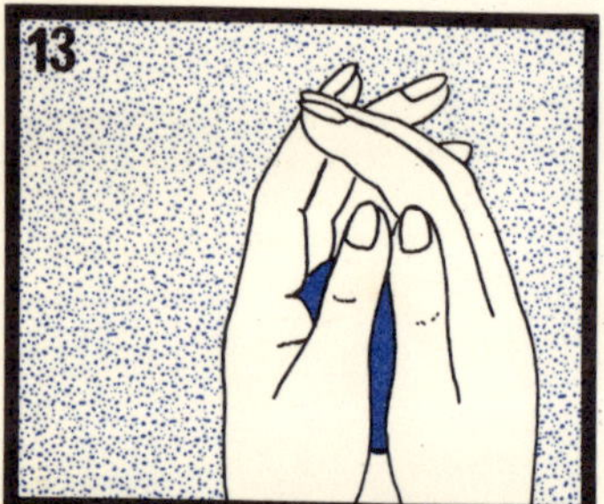

Now make the owl family. Roll a piece of clay in your hands to make a ball about the size of a golf ball.

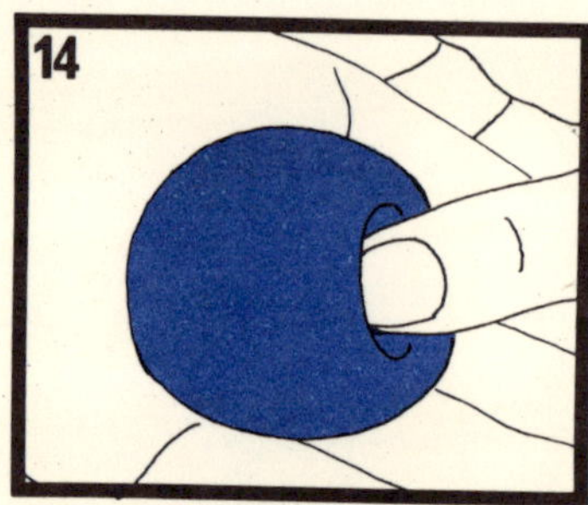

Hold ball of clay in one hand and press your thumb into the centre. Rotate clay, squeezing to an even thickness.

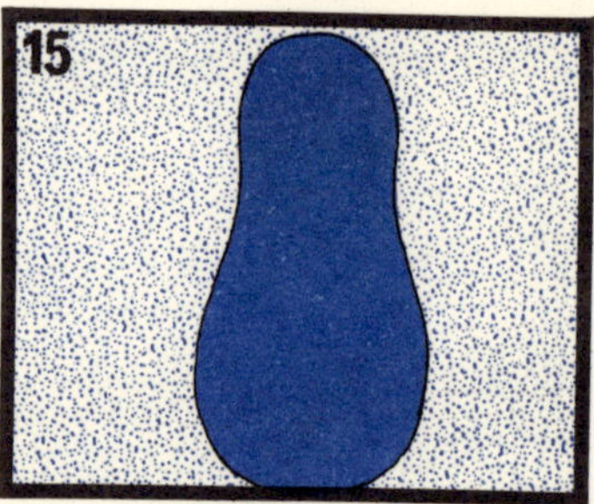

Mould ball into shape of an owl, slightly smaller at top than at the base of the body.

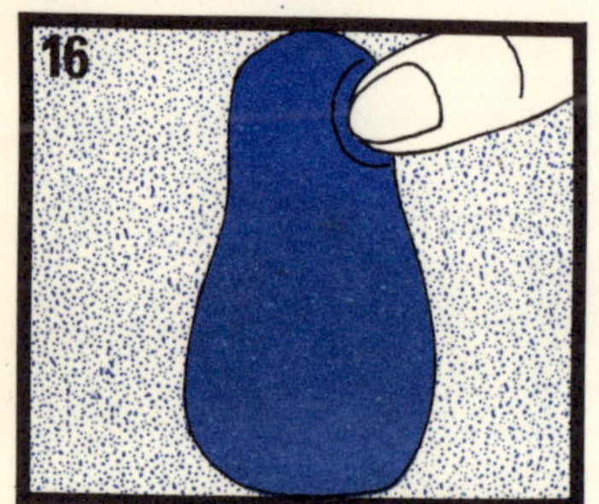

Owls have large disc-like eyes, so press in 2 hollows for the eyes and squeeze out a pointed beak.

Add details with a modelling tool or pointed stick, making realistic feather shapes on the owl's body.

To make smaller owl, roll out a piece of clay (large walnut size). Model eyes, beak and feathers as already described.

The smaller owl sits on the branch. Dampen branch and owl and press owl firmly in place. Stitch round joins; add claws.

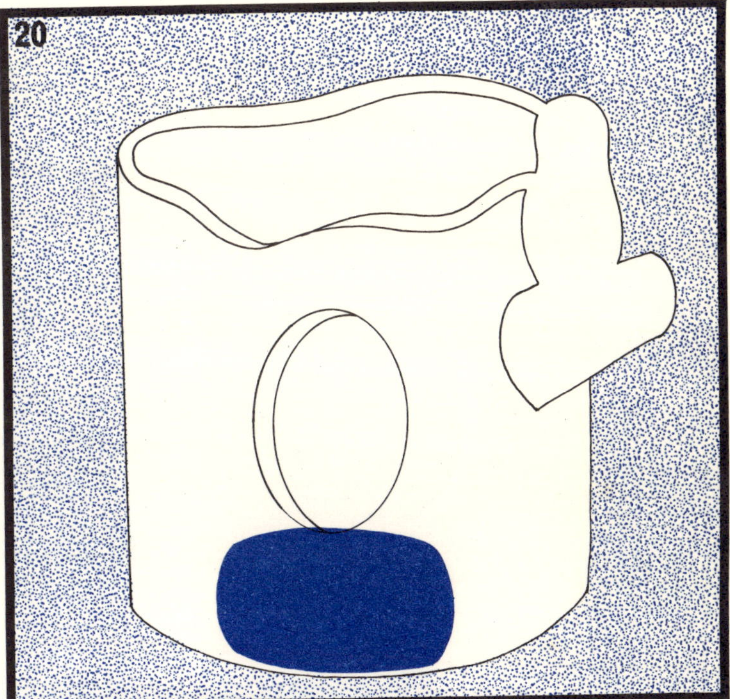

The larger owl sits by the window. For his 'perch', roll out a 'sausage' of clay and press it against the inside of the house, level with the hole. Dampen top of perch and owl's seat; press in place. Stitch round joins with modelling tool.

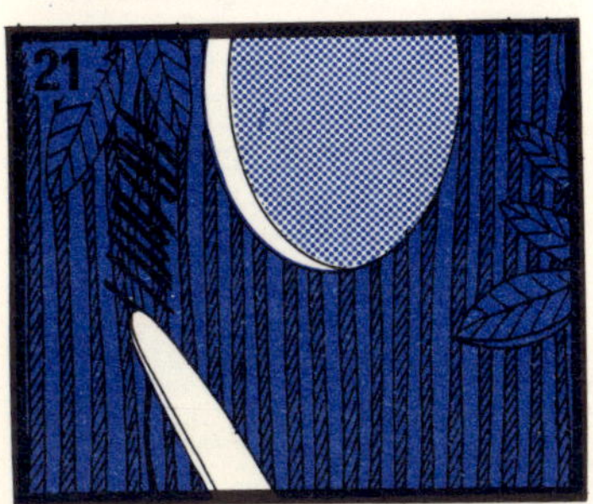

Leave lamp to dry. Watch for any cracks that might appear. If any do, dampen them and 'stitch' over again.

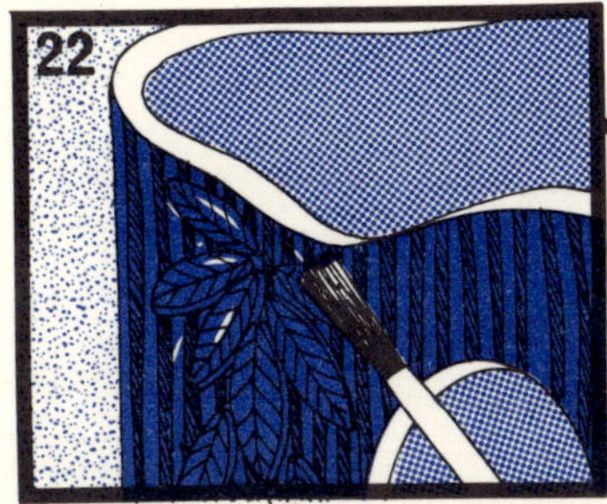

A hardener must be applied for strengthening. Mix to maker's instructions. Brush on three coats in quick succession.

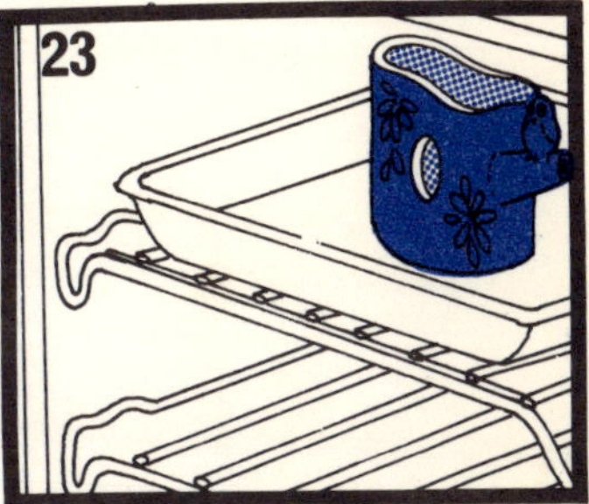

For further hardening put in a cold oven, bringing temperature up to 200°C (400°F). Turn off heat and leave to cool.

Paint with bright poster paint –(it could be mixed with emulsion paint). Finish with coat of glaze.

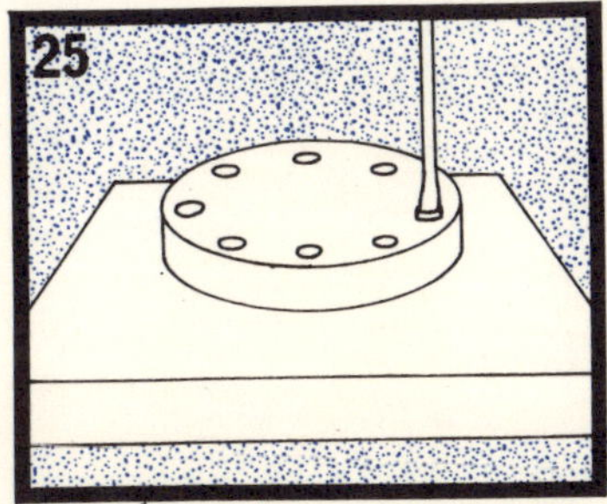

Cut a rectangular base board, larger than the model, and a circular one to fit inside the house. Screw together.

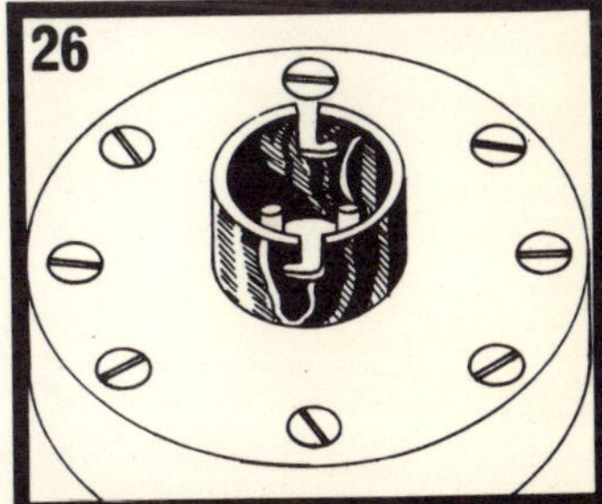

Paint base dark green. Screw lampholder to base; push clay house on top of base. Put in light bulb and switch on.

The Dye is Cast

Tie-dye is a fascinating hobby which makes fabric designers of us all. The principle is to tie the fabric before dyeing. Where it is tied the fabric will resist the dye and retain the background colour. By twisting and tying the fabric in different ways—using thin or thick string, bandages or rubber bands—you can create entirely your own patterns. Untie, retie and redye the fabric in other places and overprint a second colour. By tying in stones, coins or other small objects, you can make circles or ovals, and create those well-known 'sun burst' splashes of colour. Be as imaginative as you like: use a chart, to isolate a design like our amusing representational cat, or geometric shapes such as squares and diamonds. Give a length of tie-dyed fabric to a friend to make up into a dress or summer skirt, curtains, a bedspread or a tablecloth.

YOU WILL NEED:
1½ yds. cotton or linen, 36 ins. wide, white
1 tin each cold fabric dyes in leaf green and blue
2 sachets of cold dye-fix
8 tablespoons salt
Needle · strong thread
Pencil · polythene bag · string
Rubber gloves
7 ft length thick dowel or cane · sandpaper · saw
5 ft. cord for hanging
6 ins. piping cord for tail
Few scraps felt for features
Flower stalks for whiskers
Clear household adhesive
False eyelashes, or scrap of furnishing fringing
Large bowl or bucket
Tablespoon · wooden spoon
apron · measuring jug

If you are using new fabric, wash in hot water and detergent to remove the 'dressing'. When almost dry, iron.

Using paper drawn into 1 in. squares—newspaper will do—copy the pattern of the cat (see details on right).

The cat's outline is drawn to scale. Each square in the pattern above represents 1 1 in. square on graph paper. Draw line down the centre of the squared paper and carefully copy outline. Fold paper down line, right side out; cut out cat shape.

Draw round cat in centre of fabric. Run two rows running stitches round outline, using strong thread. Leave ends loose.

Holding the 4 ends of thread firmly, pull up running stitches until cat shape is just a bunch in the fabric.

Knot the thread ends firmly together with the material gathered tightly. Bind round the bunched outline with thread.

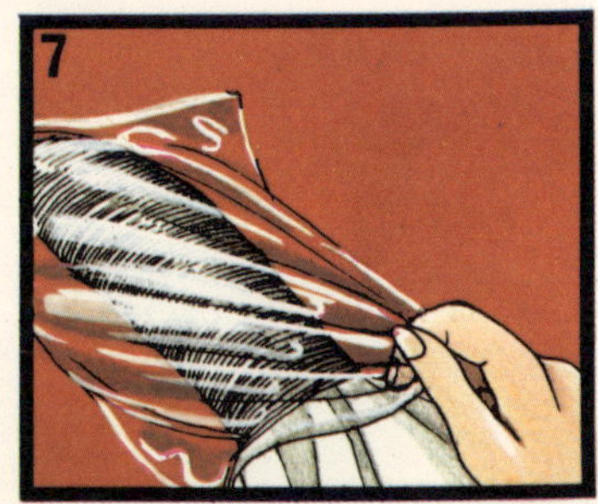

Push the bunched-up portion into small polythene bag, tie it tightly at top so that no dye will penetrate.

Cut short lengths of string. Crumple up remainder of fabric, tie all over in tight little bundles with string.

Pierce tin of dye in the first colour, (here it's leaf green); dissolve in 1 pint of warm water.

Using the wooden spoon, stir until all traces of dye powder have disappeared. Pour from jug into large bowl.

Rinse out jug, measure out 4 tablespoons household salt and 1 packet of cold dye-fix. Stir and add to dye solution.

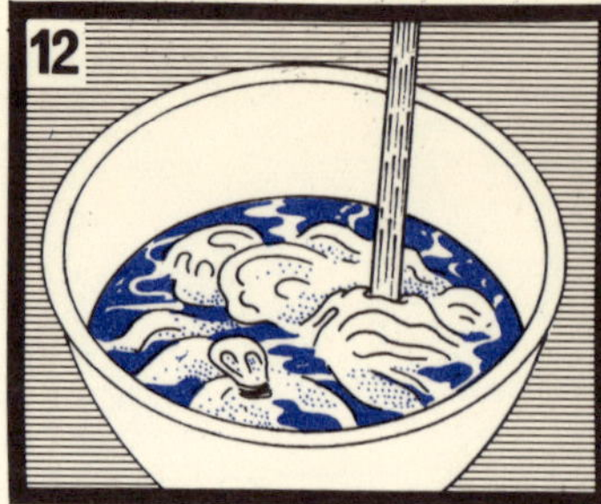

Immerse bunched-up fabric in dye for about an hour, stirring occasionally with wooden stick. (Wear an apron to do this).

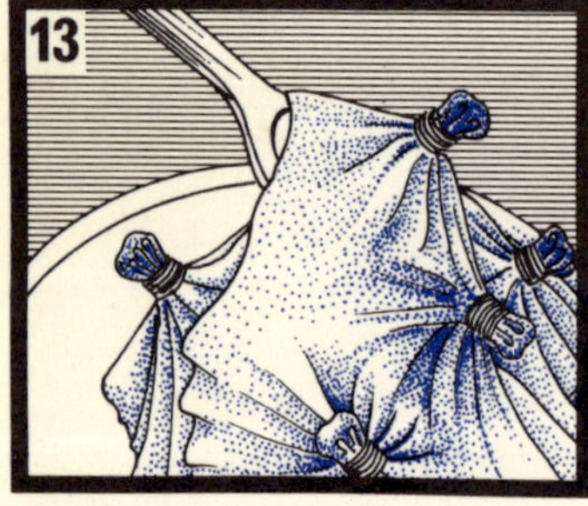

Lift the material out on end of spoon, taking care not to splash yourself. Rinse in clear water to remove surplus dye.

Undo string bindings, but do not untie top of bag. Rebunch to expose some of the white area. Retie in different places.

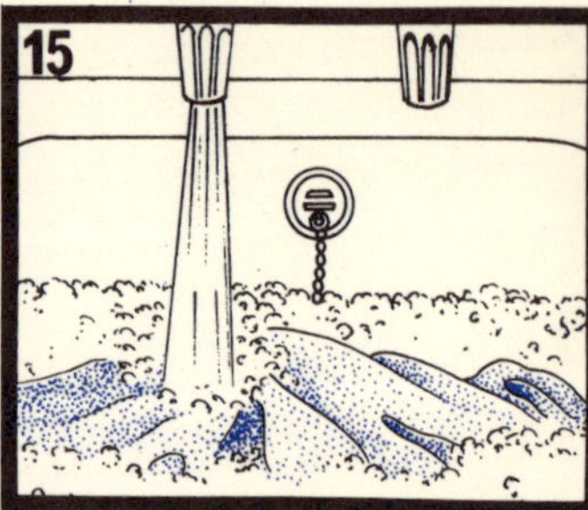

Repeat dyeing process with blue dye, mixing it up and using as already described. Rinse until water runs clear.

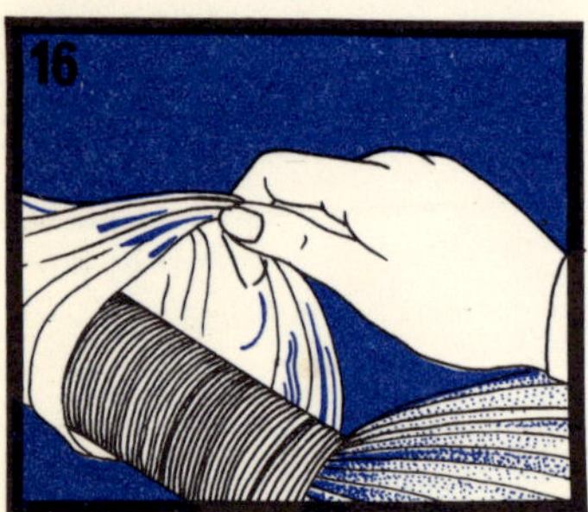

Untie strings and remove polythene bag, but not gathering-thread round cat shape. Wash in hot detergent water. Rinse.

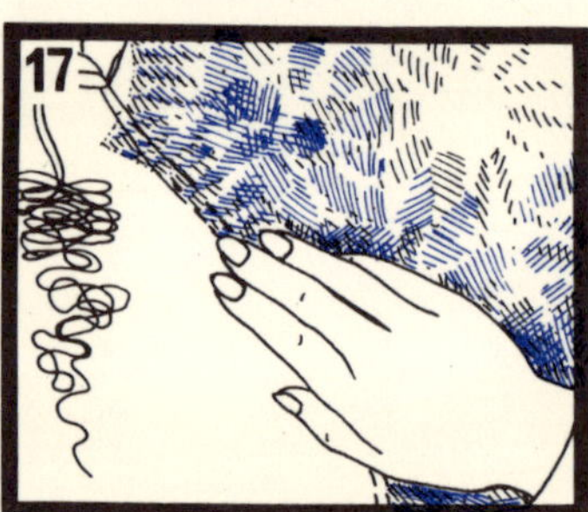

When fabric is dry, remove outline stitches. Iron with a steam iron, or leave fabric damp if ironing with non-steam.

Make tracks for poles. At top edge, turn over $\frac{1}{4}$ in. to wrong side; press. Turn 1 in. more, press and machine. Repeat at other edge.

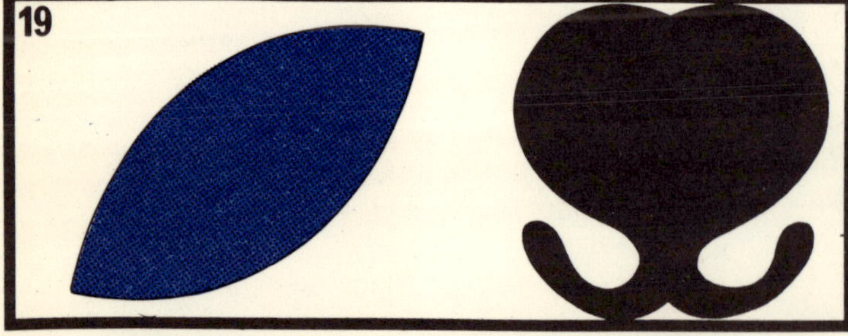

Using greaseproof paper, trace outlines of eyes and nose, above Cut out paper shapes. Pin the eye shape to olive green felt scrap and cut out. Repeat for second eye. Pin nose shape to black felt scrap and cut out, taking care with the narrow lines.

Stick on features. For whiskers, cut dried flower stalks. Apply false eyelashes, or trim scrap of dark furnishing fringe.

Tie knot in white cord for tail. Sew it firmly in place, and then at intervals. (It will prove a temptation to children.)

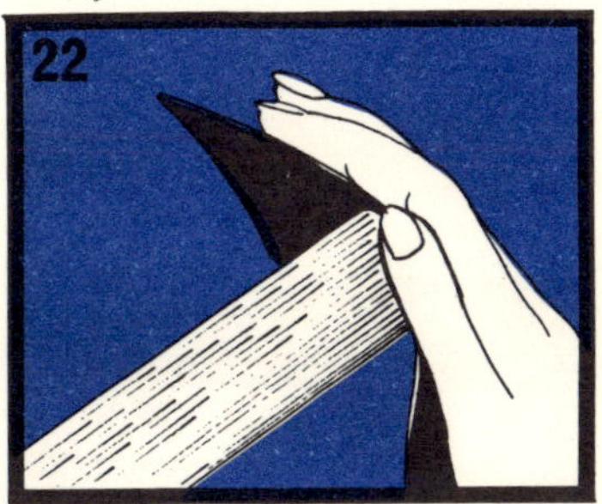

Saw pole in half, smooth off ends with sandpaper if needed. Thread one length of pole through each channel at top and bottom.

Tie firm knot in long length of cord, or sew two ends together. Wrap it round overlapping pole each side at top.

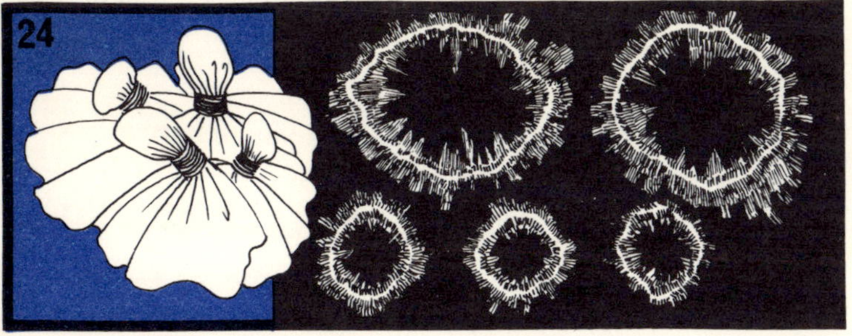

For other patterns, tie objects such as pebbles, shells or marbles into fabric. Bind tightly below them with string.

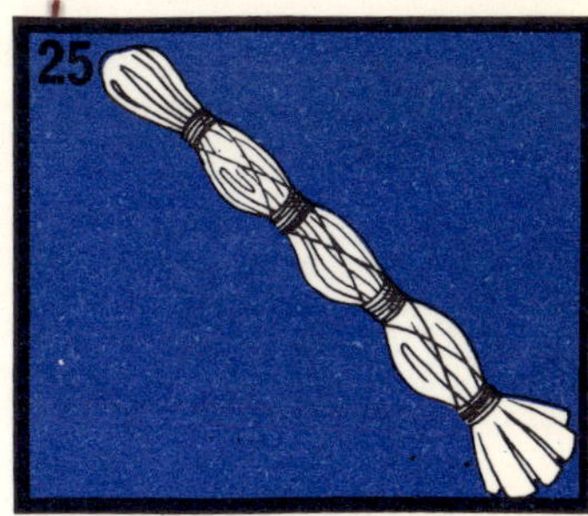

Screw fabric into a tight rope fold in middle, twist and then bind tightly with string. This is called 'twist and coil'.

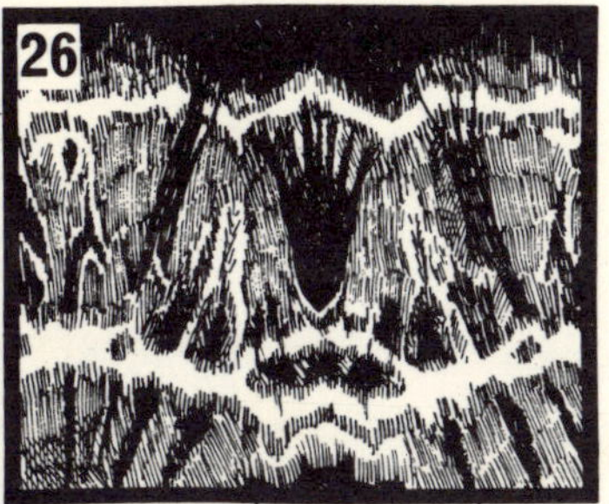

This method produces a pattern of white wavy lines, effective when fabric is to be used for a skirt, bedspread or curtains.

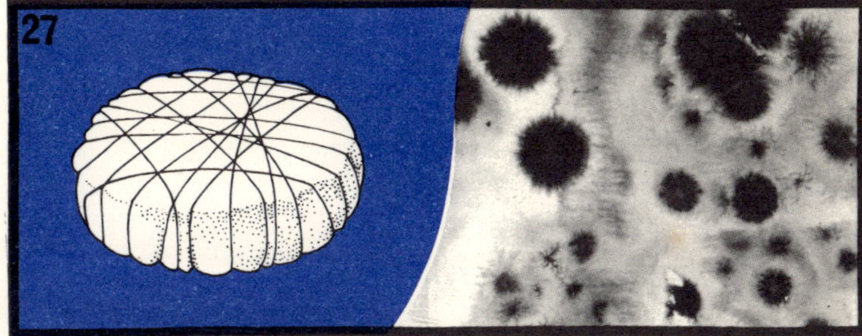

For marbling, crumple fabric in your hand into a tight ball; bind round and round. Retie in different places for the second colour.

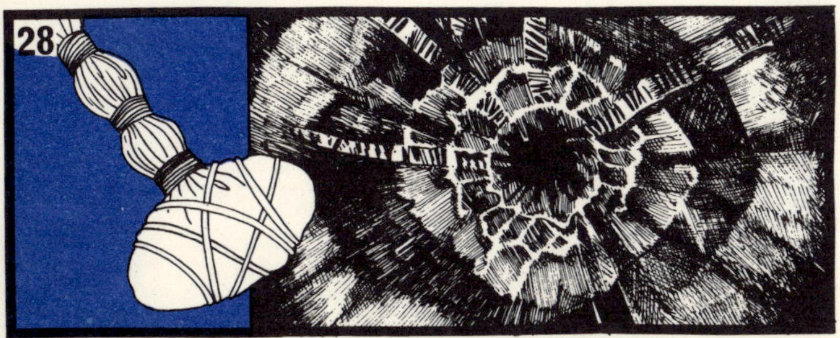

To make a sunburst, tie a stone in fabric. Bind in tightly with thread, then bind round above it at 1 in. intervals.

Try the technique used for cat outline in other ways. Try diamonds, circles, triangles and other abstract or animal shapes.

Frame Those Flowers

Flowers are always a pleasing gift, and it's a pity they ever have to wither and die. Yet here's an idea which will enable you to give your family and friends a beautiful 'permanent bouquet': dried flower pictures. You certainly don't need to be an artist to create them, although an eye for balance and design does help. Unlike pressed flower pictures, those using dried materials (see pages 38/39 for 'drying' instructions) do not need glass in the frame. Cut a piece of strong card to fit the inside measure of the frame, cover it with a subtle print or a coloured plain fabric, and plan a nosegay, a swirl of falling leaves or a pretty posy. Superimpose light colours on to dark ones, matt textures on top of shiny ones. The real art in this hobby is in avoiding overcrowding the picture and in knowing when each carefully chosen flower or leaf is shown at its best.

YOU WILL NEED:
Old picture frame (without glass)
Piece of strong card to fit inside measurement
Fabric about 2ins. larger all round than card backing
Scissors
Needle and strong thread
Craft knife · steel rule · pencil
Colourless household adhesive
Tweezers for handling small plant material
Collection of dried and preserved flowers, grasses, leaves and seedheads

Cut piece of card to fit frame. Cut fabric 2 ins. larger all round. Cover card, mitre corners, stitch across at back.

Begin the design with a strong feature–such as the 7 preserved (almost black) laurel leaves. Place as shown.

When you are satisfied with the way you have arranged them, stick in place, using the adhesive sparingly.

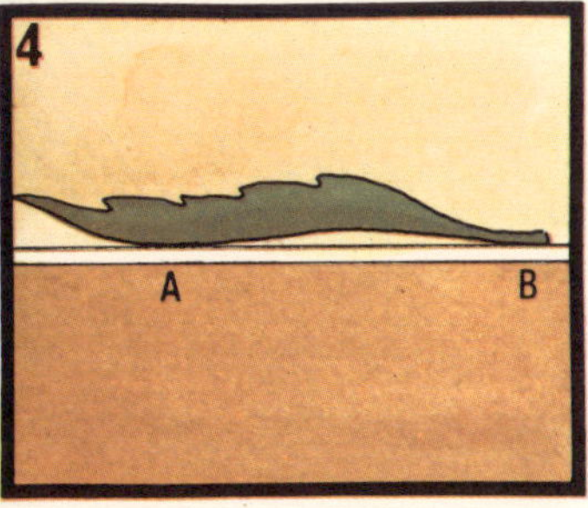

Try each flower or leaf against flat surface to test exactly where it will touch. Lightly apply adhesive to 'touch spot'.

Using tweezers, place the 2 curving lines of dyed grass-heads making a strong oval shape beneath the laurel leaves.

Glue a red dried hydrangea floret a greeny one, a dried poppy seedhead and a pink acrolinium to each laurel leaf.

On the centre laurel leaf, glue a large helichrysum flower and four tiny acrolinium buds. Above and below place hydrangea florets.

At each side, a large and a small helichrysum flower, two lupin pods and tiny sprays of dried rue seedheads curving up.

Sprigs of preserved cupressus make a feature. On top are snippets of rue; purple and cream love-in-a-mist seedheads.

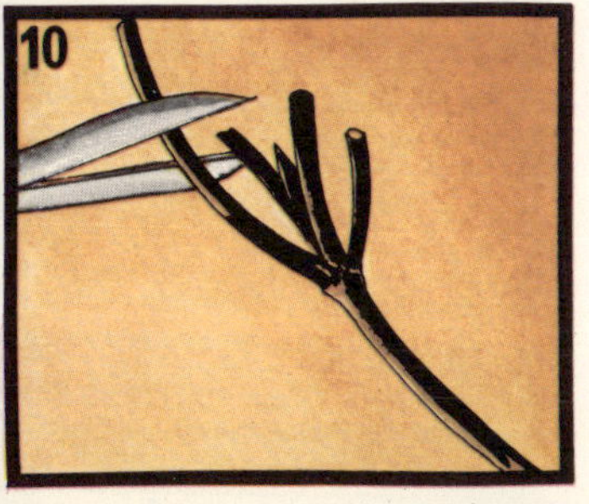

The laurel stalks, also jet black, make upward sweeps either side. Above them are black grassheads.

A picture is more interesting if it is not symmetrical. Furry heads of hare's tailgrass and preserved ivy leaves hang down.

Split lupin seedpods; alternate with lower laurel leaves; below them, fat heads of dried lavender, and two single black grassheads.

Nursery Mobile

A new baby in the family—or in a friend's family—always presents an opportunity for the more industrious to aim their talents in the little one's direction, especially as 'baby presents' are so expensive to buy. Usually the offerings take the form of either knitted bootees, bonnets and so on, or soft, cuddly toys. But why not be original? Here's a lovely nursery mobile that will not only amuse the baby but also prove an attractive addition to the playroom. You can include his or her name as part of the decoration, and if the blocks are sealed and varnished the screw eyes can be taken out later so that the cubes can be used as building blocks.

YOU WILL NEED:
Piece of selected $1\frac{1}{2} \times 1\frac{1}{2}$ in. pine, 15 ins. long
18 small screweyes
Wooden dowel 3/16 in. diameter, 3 ft. long
Decorative scraps and letters
2 yds. coloured embroidery thread, fine decorative string or knitting wool
Fuse wire
Clear varnish or non-toxic paint
White card
8 stick-on miniature mirror tiles, each about $\frac{3}{4}$ in. sq., or large sequins

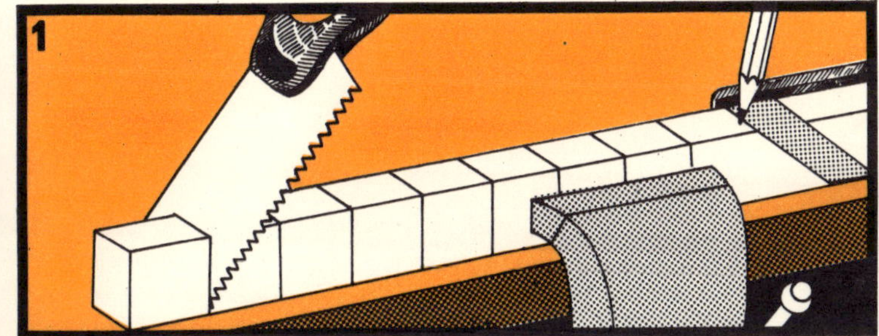

Take the pine and mark it very accurately on all faces at $1\frac{1}{2}$ in. intervals, using pencil and set square. Then with a tenon saw cut it into cubes. Sand smooth.

Draw a diagonal on each cube to find the centres for screweyes. Begin hole with a nail or bradawl, then screw in the eyes.

Varnish or paint cubes. Stick on letters and pictures and varnish over. Tie a length of thread through each screweye.

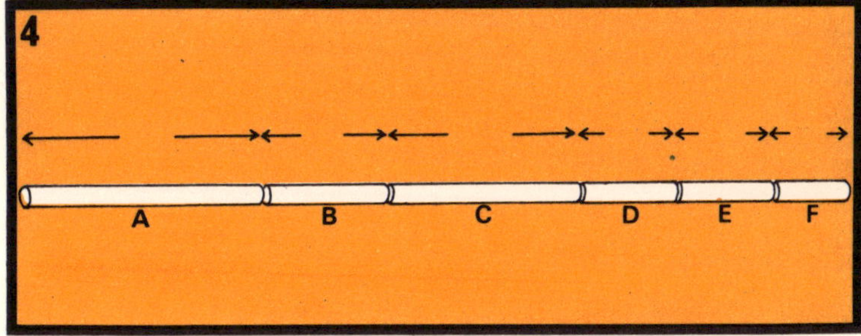

Next cut the length of dowel into strips, making them the following lengths as shown in the diagram: (a)–$7\frac{3}{4}$ ins.; (b)–4 ins.; (c)–$6\frac{1}{4}$ ins.; (d)–$3\frac{1}{4}$ ins.; (e)–$3\frac{1}{4}$ ins.; (f)–$2\frac{1}{2}$ ins.

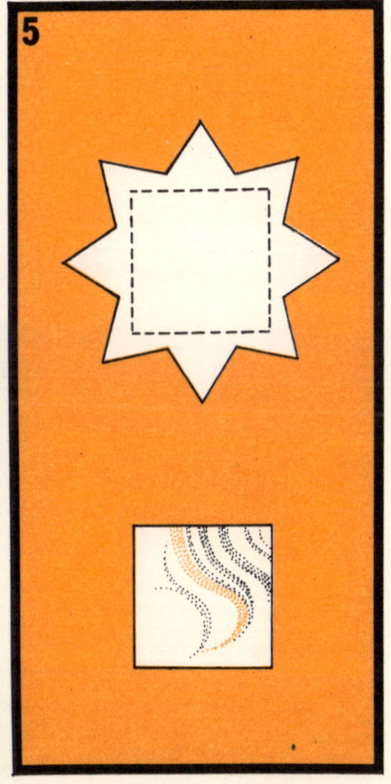

Cut out 4 $1\frac{1}{2}$ in. squares of card. Paint silver and glue in pairs. Glue a mirror tile or sequins in the centre of each side.

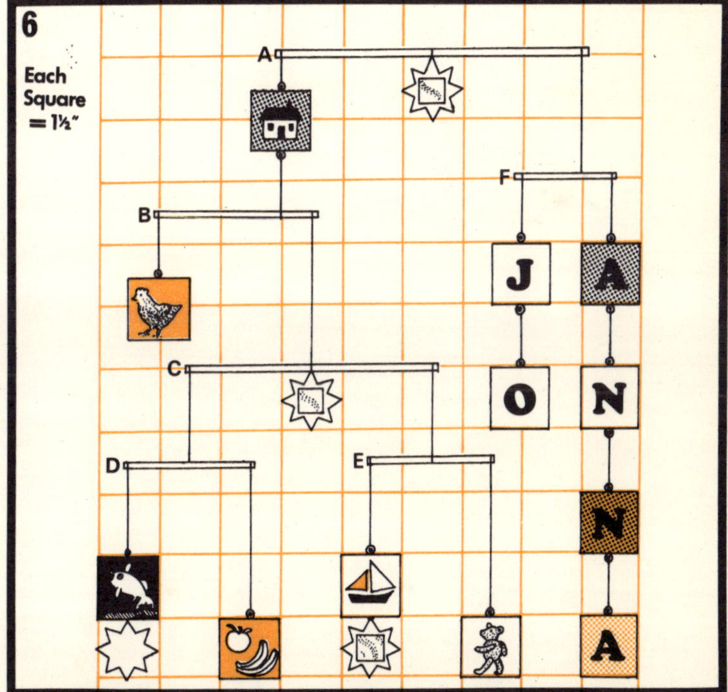

Twist short bits of wire into figure of 8 shapes. Slip 1 on each dowel. Tie threads from cubes to dowels (d) and (e), (follow lengths shown). Check balance sliding wire until dowel hangs horizontally. Twist wire to fix. Repeat with (b), (c), (a) and (f).

Arty 'Antiques'

And now for a little decoupage—a very old craft, dating back almost 3,000 years. Basically it's the technique of decoratively mounting cut-out or torn paper motifs and pictures on boards, trays, boxes, furniture, etc., and sealing or 'sinking' them, using transparent varnish. It was practised in France and Italy in the 18th century and became very popular in England. The name comes from the French 'decouper', 'to cut', and not only can cut-out prints be used on their own, they can be combined to form a collage or 'trompe l'oeil' [eye-deceiving] design. Prints can also be torn and 'distressed' for an antique effect and natural objects such as leaves, feathers and pressed flowers can be incorporated. Follow the instructions to create your own simple or more complicated picture.

YOU WILL NEED:
Piece of smooth, prepared wood about $\frac{1}{2}$ in. thick
Selection of prints, etc. for trompe l'oeil picture or single print for simple picture
Decoupage antiquing finish (or brown varnish or paint)
Decoupage finish (polyurethane or picture varnish)
Sealer for prints (not always necessary)
Brushes · white spirit adhesive
Kitchen paper towel

To mount a torn-out print, paint board with antiquing liquid, decoupage colour or clear varnish along wood grain. Leave to dry.

Tear the print irregularly around the edge, always tearing away from you, and then sand round edges on back to make them thin and ragged.

Spread glue on print back, if necessary, thinning with water to give a smooth coat.

Place print exactly in correct position and rub down flat from centre to express air bubbles and remove all wrinkles.

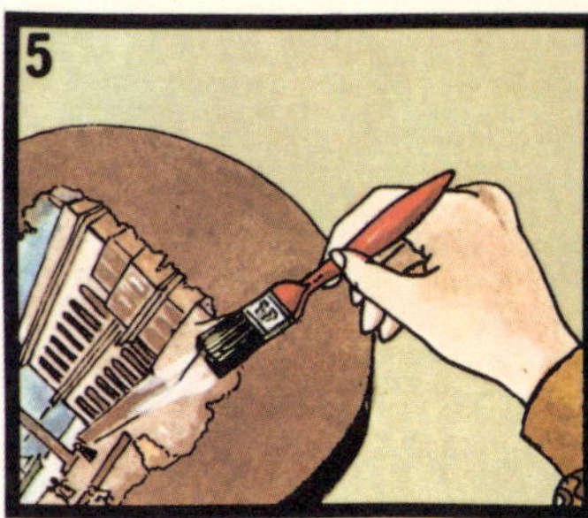

Test corner of print with finish or varnish. If picture blurs, seal first with picture sealer. Apply coat of finish or varnish.

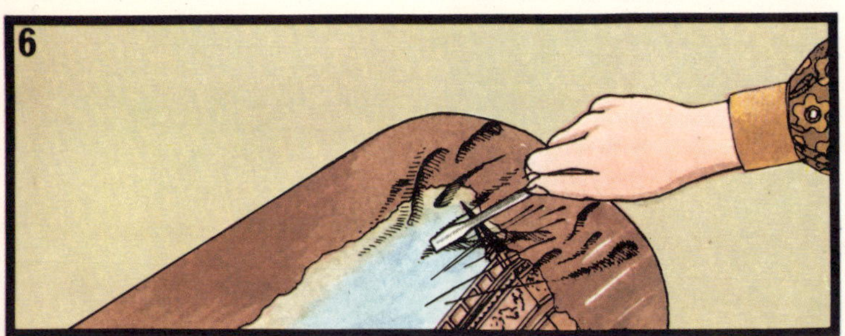

If you would like an 'antique' look to your decoupage, dent and scratch the surface with screwdriver. Dig out small chips of wood from round the edge.

Apply antiquing glaze or varnish to surface. After 5 minutes partly wipe away with soft cloth. Leave most glaze round edges.

When dry, apply coat of clear finish. Allow to dry, then rub surface with steel wool and polish with a soft cloth.

For another effect, mount the print on a plain colour background; instead of an antique appearance—just treat it with clear finish.

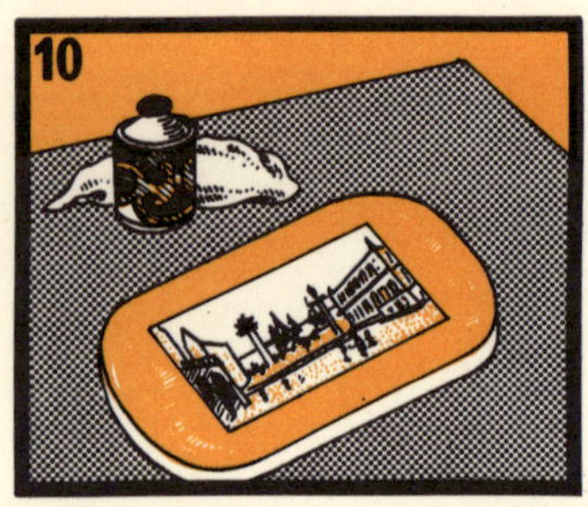

Use a small amount of furniture polish and rub over finished picture. Leave for a few minutes, then buff with soft cloth.

To make 'trompe l'oeil' picture, pick a selection of interesting prints and cut them out. Choose a background board and paint it.

Move prints around until you have an interesting design. They may be placed amusingly, formally or overlapping one another. Glue down print. If overlapping, stick larger ones first. Ferns, feathers, pressed leaves, etc. may be incorporated.

If necessary seal prints on test, then coat all over with one layer of finish. Allow to dry.

Add trompe l'oeil shadow effect. Imagine light source and where shadows would fall on your picture if objects were solid.

Using antique glaze or dark varnish, paint a 'shadow' down the side of each cut out, opposite the 'light source'.

Thick shadows make objects appear far away: if you paint in thin shadows they will seem to be much closer.

Allow 'shadows' to dry thoroughly, then finish with two clear coats of finish or varnish and polish up as before.

Decoupage technique is an effective way of displaying cigarette cards, theatre programmes, postcards etc.

A flower still-life may be cut out with curved nail scissors, pieces rearranged, mounted and 'sunk' in clear finish.

Before cutting, join delicate parts of pattern with coloured pencil 'ladder' lines. Cut ladder parts when ready to glue.

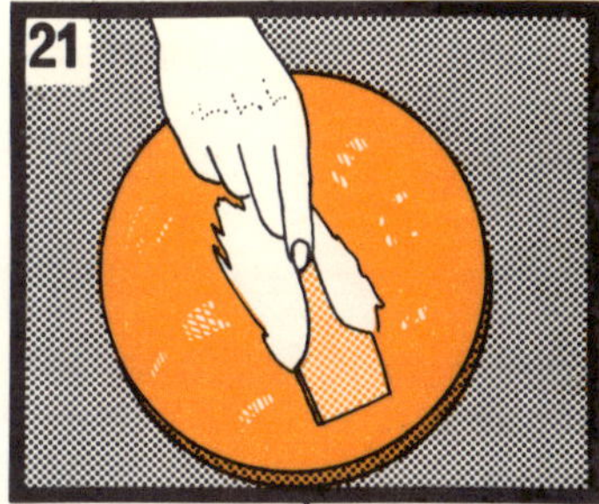

Prepare background with suitable decoupage colour. When dry, smooth glue where print will go. Cut out ladder parts.

Carefully position cut-outs with tweezers. Gently mop up excess glue with damp towel. Press cut-out firmly down.

Sink print by building up layers of finish. Apply 6 coats, allowing each to dry before next is put on. Sand down with fine sandpaper, being careful not to sand any of the print. Wipe off the sanding dust with a soft cloth.

Apply 2 more coats of finish, allow to dry, then repeat sanding process. Continue until surface is quite flat (so no print edges protrude when you run your finger over it). This may mean putting on up to 20 coats of finish.

Apply final coat of finish. For glossy surface, wax polish. For matt finish, rub with steel wool. Rub up with soft cloth.

Beautiful pictures, box decorations, etc. may be made from pressed leaves, flowers, ferns and feathers. Sink as directed.

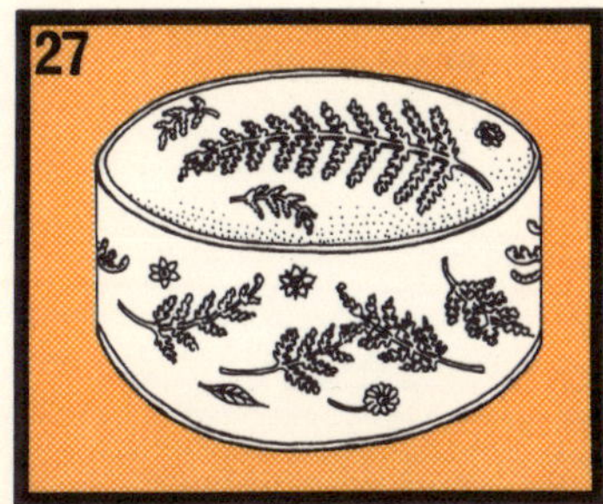

Paint background, arrange and stick on leaves, etc., then paint with layers of finish. Many layers may be needed.

Gold filigree is attractive as a decoupage material. If unobtainable, motifs from a gold doyley make a good substitute.

Tame Tiger

We're all children at heart, so this lovable, cuddly tiger, although basically intended as a baby's toy, could double as a cushion for a teenager's 'pad'—or equally well be at home in any lounge or sitting room as a 'fun' decoration. The tiger shown here has a benevolent look on his face, but of course you can alter the pattern to suit your own ideas. Equally, you could adapt the basic idea to make a bear, lion or any other animal of your choice. But first a word of warning: do not leave any large, cushion-like soft toy in the cot with a very young baby—it could be as dangerous as a pillow.

YOU WILL NEED:
Two pieces of fur fabric, each 17×17 ins.
Kapok or synthetic stuffing material
Zip fastener (15 ins.)
Small pieces of felt or cotton fabric in red, black, green and brown
Matching sewing thread.

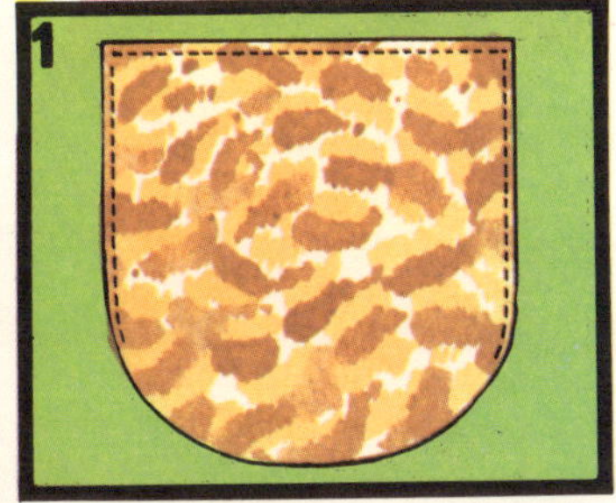

Place fabric pieces together, right sides facing; curve bottom corners as shown. Machine round three sides.

Cut out in felt: 1 nose piece, 2 eyelash pieces, 2 black pupils; 2 green eye pieces; 1 red mouth and nose; 2 brown ears; 6 straight black whiskers $\frac{1}{4} \times 4$ ins. Turn fabric cushion pieces right side out.

Pin features on one side of fabric. Stitch each one in place, using matching thread and small stitches.

Embroider a white highlight on each eye pupil and a group of red dots on the nose piece, using French knots (see no. 5).

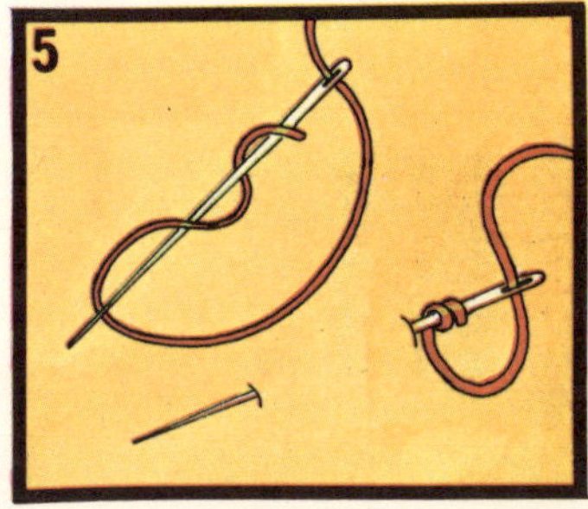

Form a French knot as shown in diagram, inserting needle, winding thread twice round, and pulling it through.

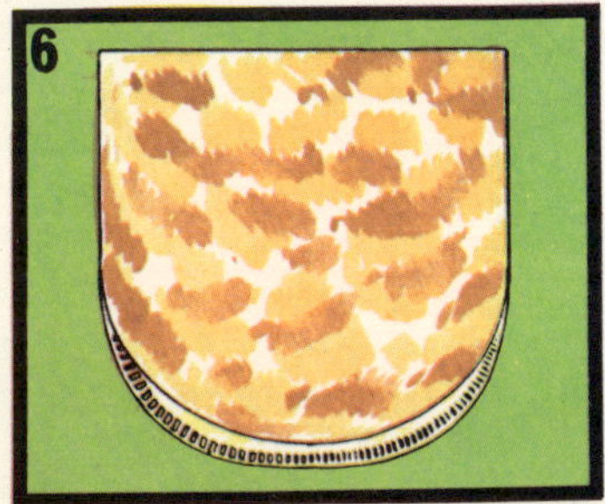

Tack, then machine or back stitch the zip fastener in place on the curved section of the cushion.

Stuff cushion toy with kapok or other filling until it is firm but not too hard. Close zip to complete.

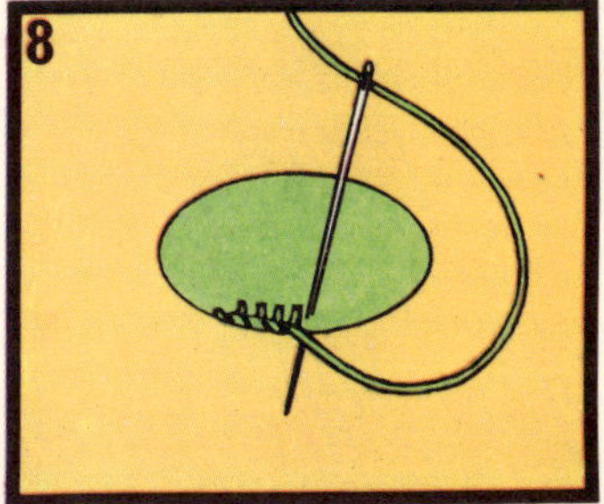

If you prefer to use scraps of cotton for the features, buttonhole them in place, as shown in the diagram.

A Mouse About The House

A mascot for a teenager, an ornament for a mantelshelf – even a pin cushion for grandmother. This checked mouse is one of the most versatile of presents. As one of Nature's more caricaturable creatures, the mouse crops up in all shapes, sizes and substances – hence the steadily growing trend to collect mouse toys. If you know a 'mouse crazy' collector, then this adorable little chap is sure to find a proud position among the collection. Children will love him too! Vary the mouse's trimmings to suit your own taste, and you can even adapt the pattern size to make a whole mouse family!

YOU WILL NEED:
Strong cotton fabric, 10×13 ins. (suggest gingham)
Piece of felt 6×6 ins.
Card for base
Darning wool for whiskers and nose
2 $\frac{5}{8}$ in. diameter buttons
Kapok or other stuffing
Lace daisies and flowers for trimming
Matching thread

Cut body piece—$11\frac{3}{4} \times 4\frac{1}{4}$ ins., tail piece—$11\frac{3}{4} \times 1\frac{1}{4}$ ins., 4 fabric ear pieces, 2 felt ear pieces—all $2\frac{1}{4}$ ins. diameter circles, 1 felt and 1 card base—$3\frac{3}{4}$ ins. diameter circle. Leave $\frac{1}{4}$ in. seam allowance round body and ear piece.

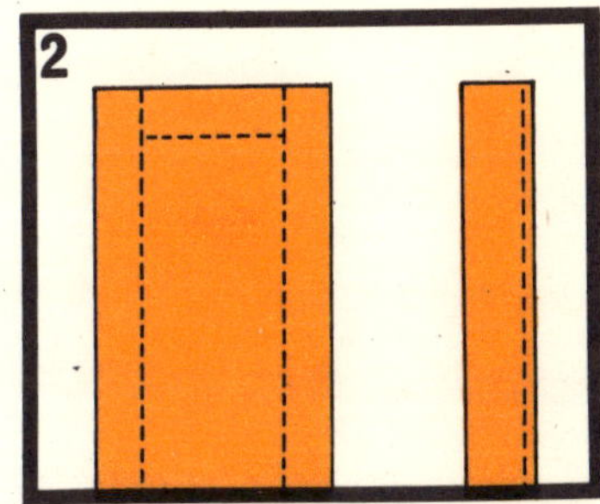

Press $\frac{1}{4}$ in. all round tail inwards, then fold in half and overstitch the edges or machine together.

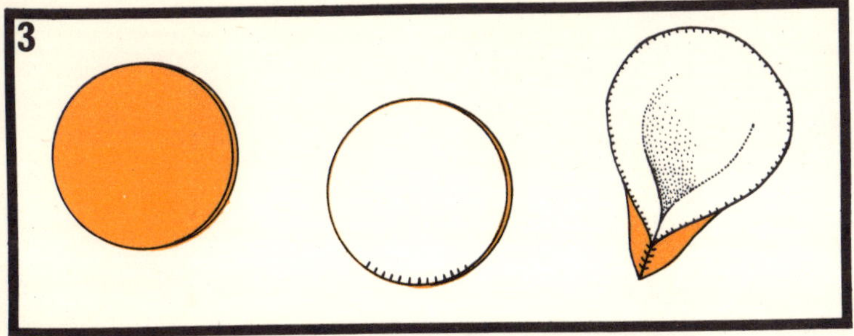

For each ear, take 2 fabric pieces. Right sides facing, sew all round, leaving $1\frac{1}{4}$ in. opening. Turn right side out, press and sew opening. Oversew 1 felt ear piece round each fabric piece. Fold ear in half and stitch edges as shown to form ear shape.

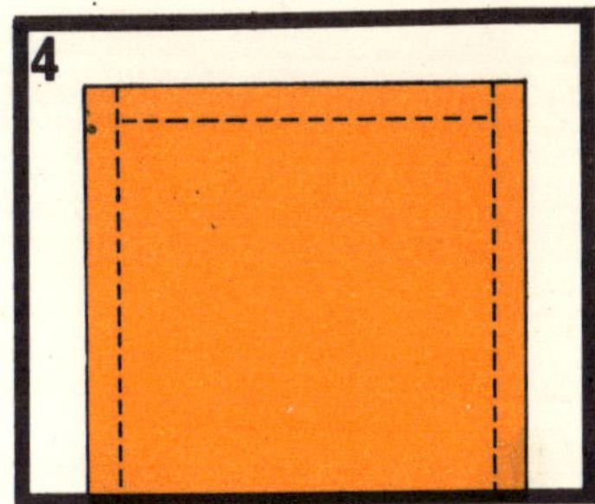

Press in $\frac{1}{2}$ in. all round body piece as shown.

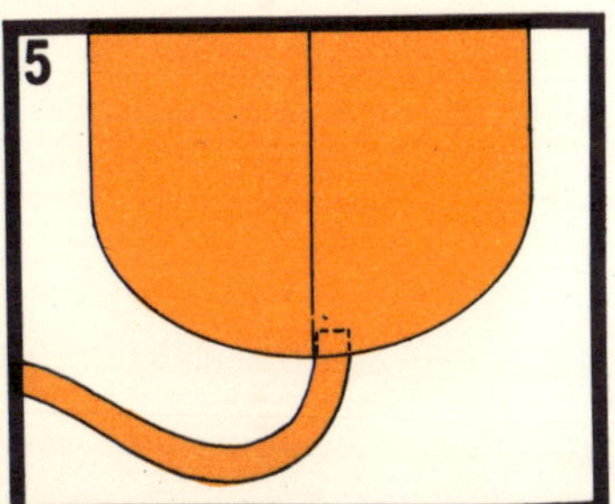

Oversew body to base, inserting the end of the tail. Sew up vertical seam to form a cylinder.

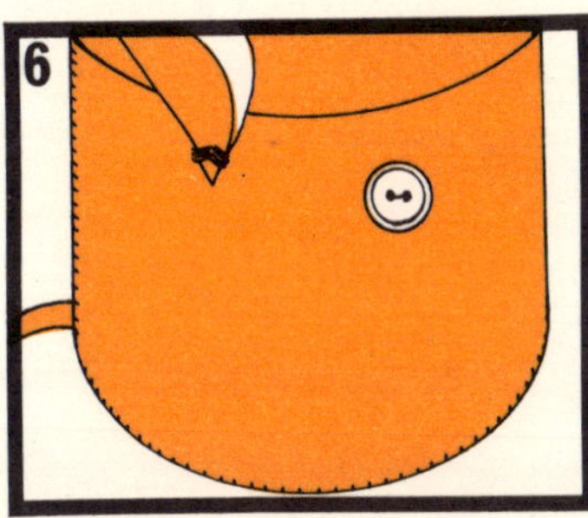

Sew on ears and eyes as shown. Stitch ears 4 or 5 times in both directions to make sure they are firm.

Place card base in bottom and stuff mouse until very full. Sew top seam just past ears, (add more stuffing if needed).

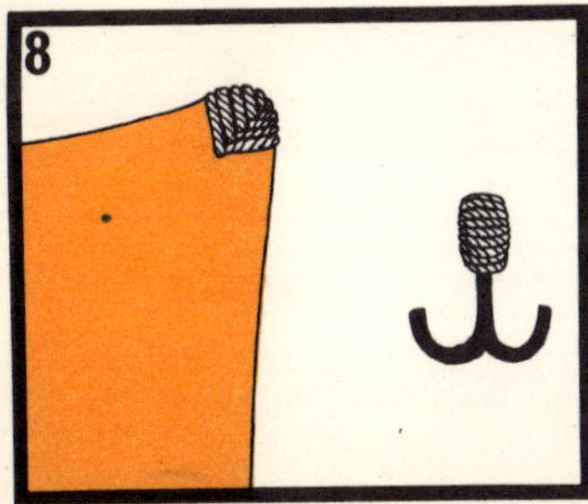

With dark wool and darning needle, oversew nose at point farthest from ears. Draw on mouth in felt-tip pen.

To make whiskers, sew 3 lengths of wool right through face leaving 2 in. lengths at each side. Knot and trim.

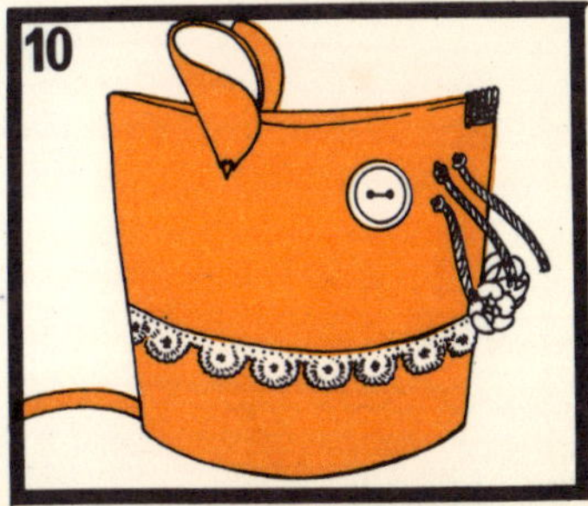

Oversew lace trimming, all round, about 2 ins. up from base. Sew on 2 artificial flowers, for decoration.

An Old Craft Revived

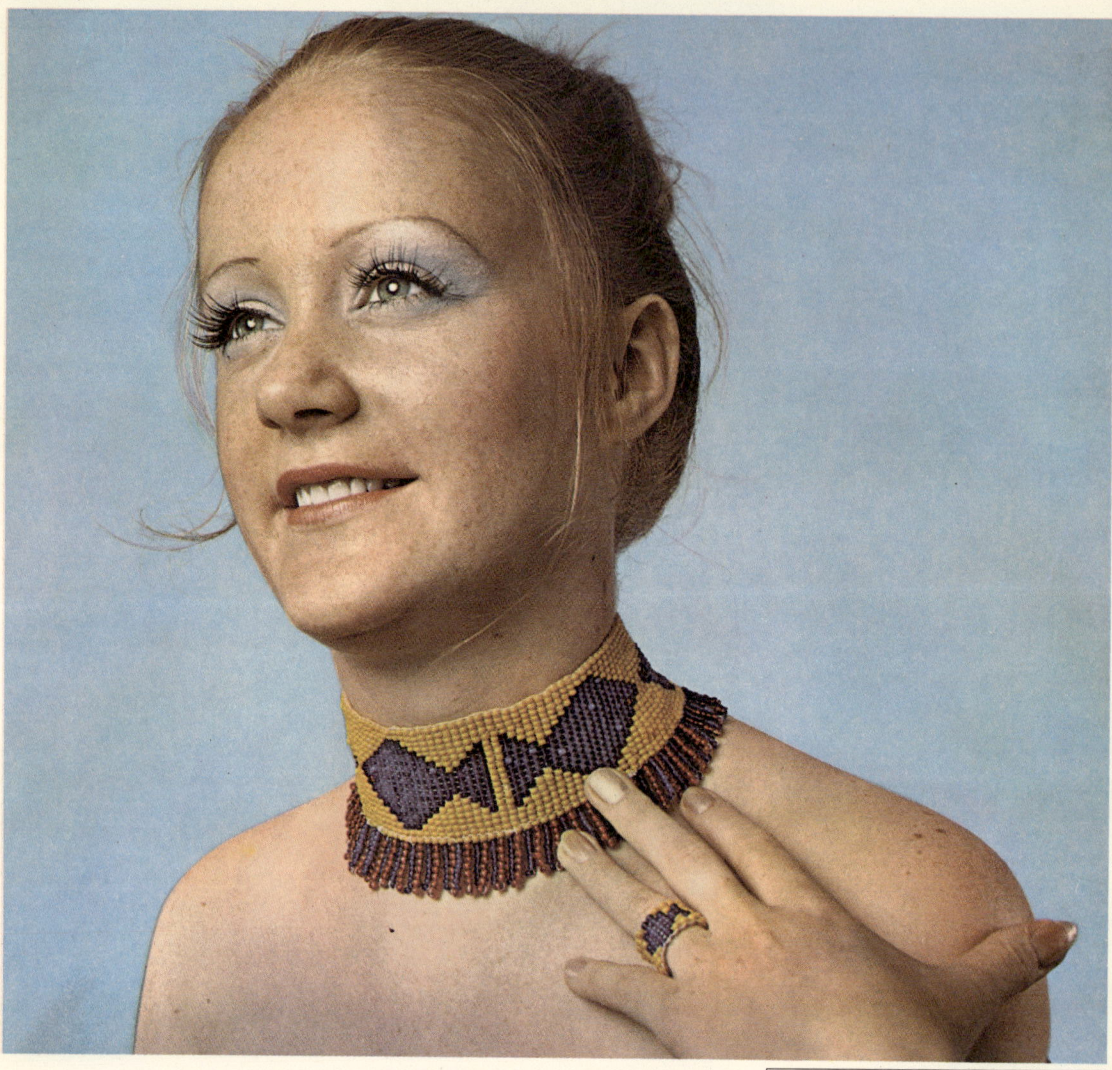

The craft of weaving beads on a small loom was once practised among the North American Indian tribes—and now it is enjoying widespread and well-deserved popularity. From basically simple techniques, many lovely objects can be produced, ranging from necklaces, rings and belts to bags, purses and mats. On these pages are instructions for making a simple bead loom at home and for weaving a wide-fringed choker and matching ring. Remember that for weaving any article you need a pattern or weaving chart to follow. Take this from a book on beading, or work out your own design. You can also copy a cross-stitch design into bead work by using a different coloured bead instead of thread, for each stitch.

YOU WILL NEED:
A beadloom, either bought or made at home from a cardboard box or a wooden box and nails
Strong linen thread
A fine beading needle
2 boxes each of yellow, blue and red small beads
Yellow ribbon
Small piece of tape

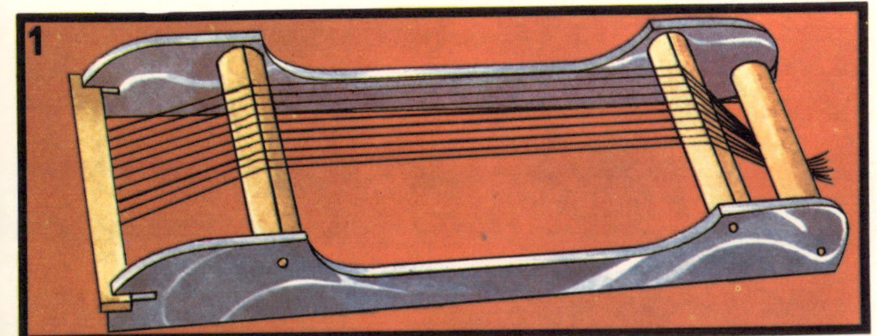

On a bought loom (above) the warp or lengthways threads are stretched across the loom and held firm at each end. Cut threads twice length needed, loop over bar and fix in slotted bar at other end. (Thread 2 warps at sides for firmness.)

To make loom, take out sides of wooden box; hammer in tacks. Wind 1 thread very tightly round all tacks as shown.

Alternatively, use a cardboard box. Take out sides; cut notches for threading. Thread with 1 long thread as before.

Above is another simple type of loom. Glue wooden strips to a piece of chipboard; knock in nails to hold warp.

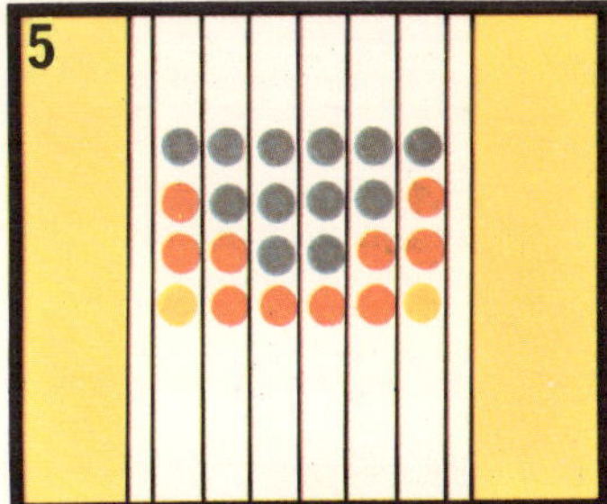

When threading on warp, allow 1 more thread than number of beads across design, plus 2 extra to reinforce side warps.

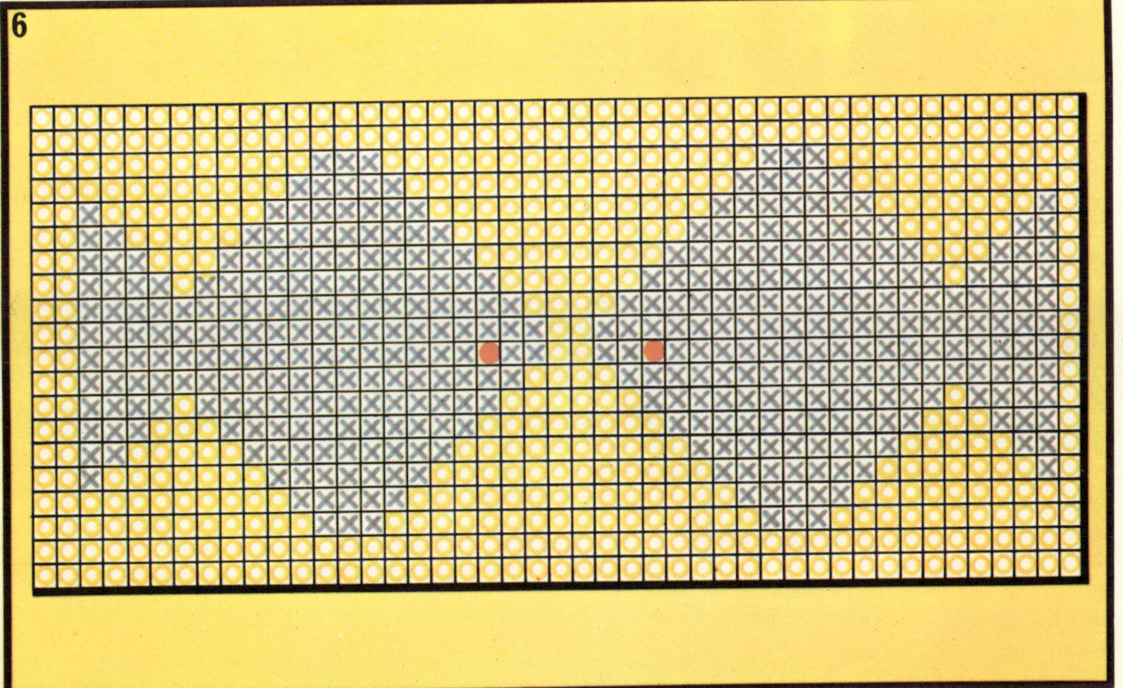

For our 'fish choker', copy the design above in any 3 colours, or vary it by putting in stripes of a fourth colour. Set 23 warp threads on to the loom (this allows for the extra at the sides). Warp length should be $10\frac{3}{4}$ ins. for the actual design of 4 fish, plus another 10 ins. Repeat the 2 facing fish pattern again to give an overall design of 4 fish.

Keep beads sorted into separate colours for ease of working. Keep pattern chart where you can easily see it.

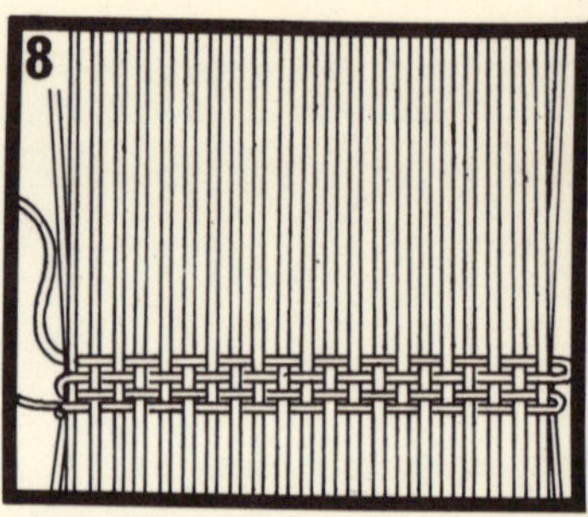

Thread needle and tie to outer side warps on left. Weave 4 lines under and over warp with weft thread.

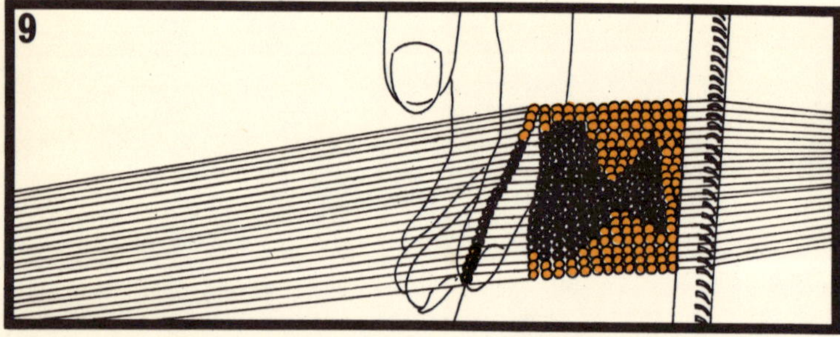

Thread the same number of beads as there are spaces between the warp threads (21), following pattern for colour. Push beads up between threads, using fingers of left hand and pressing them from underneath.

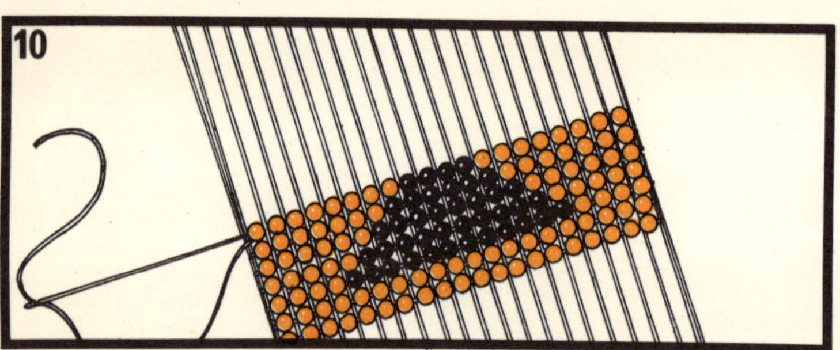

Pass needle and thread back *through* beads *over* warp threads so that the beads are held firmly in place. Thread on next line of beads and repeat the pushing up of the weft and the threading back as before.

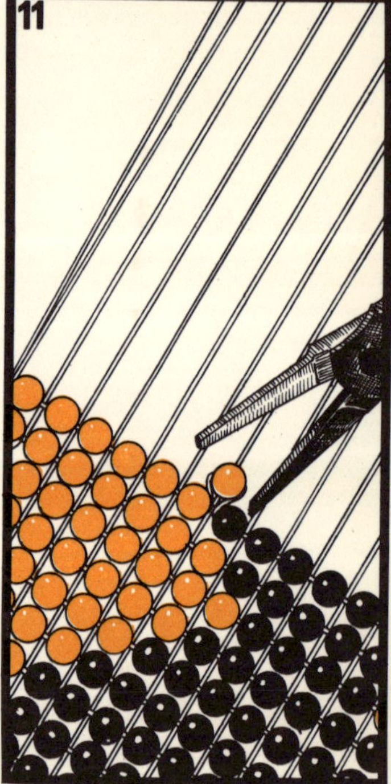

If you thread an extra bead by mistake, clip it off with pliers, being careful not to cut the thread.

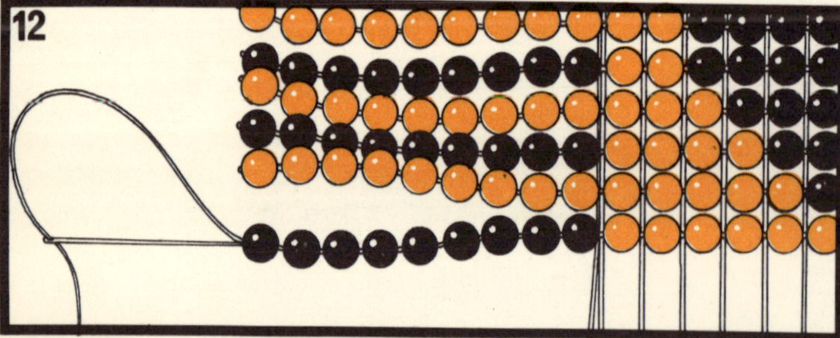

Make a side fringe at one end of each row by adding an extra nine or ten beads to the beads in each row. Turn, take thread round the last bead as a 'stopper', and run weft through all beads as shown.

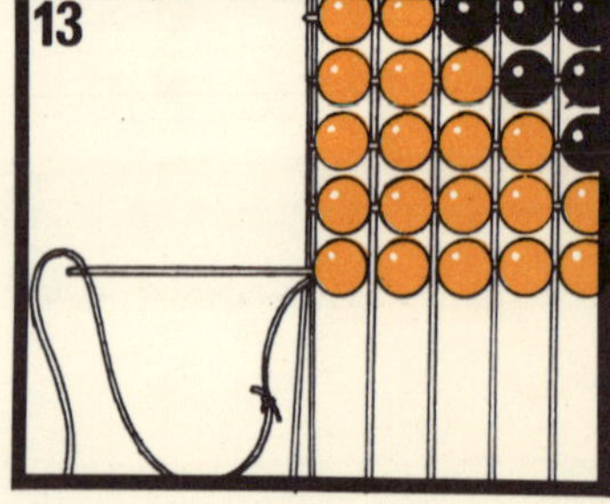

When you need to join a new length of weft, make a knot to come in the middle of a *returning* row.

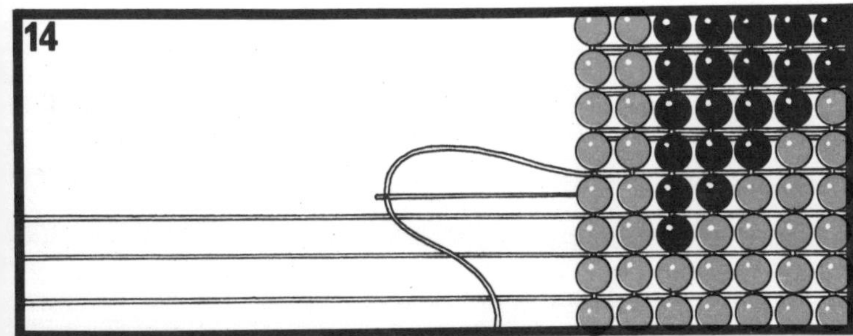

When you have completed the pattern, take the weft thread back through previous rows until it is finished. Snip off end. Remove warp threads from loom singly, thread on needle and take back through bead rows. Snip off any loose ends.

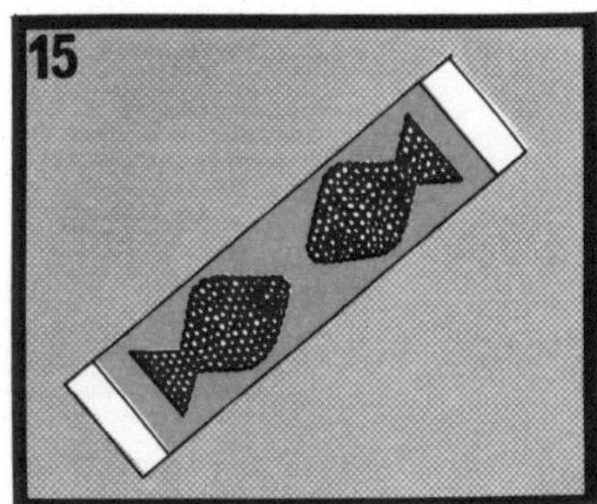

Stick small piece of ribbon or tape underneath at each end, using epoxy resin adhesive, or sew lightly to beads.

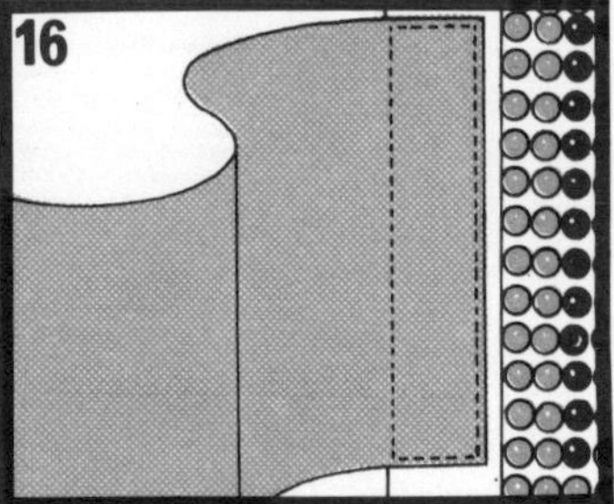

Sew a length of ribbon (to match 1 of colours) to tape at each side to tie round neck. (Tape will take the 'pull').

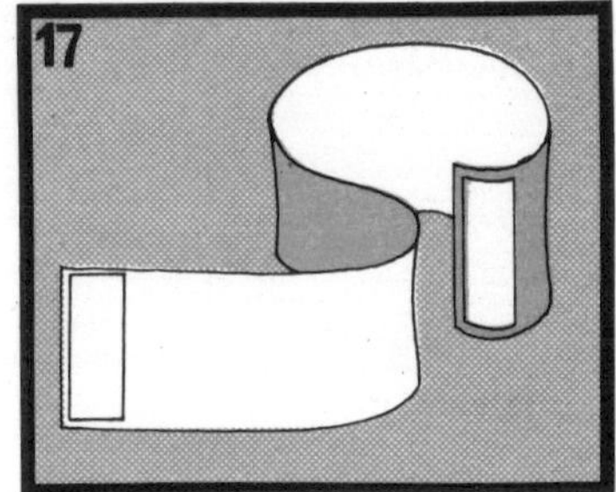

If preferred, weave choker to exact neck measurement, plus 1 in. Sew Velcro fastening at each end.

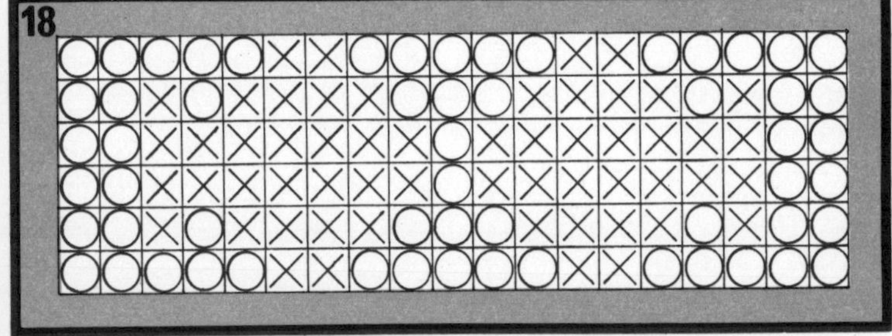

To make matching ring, set on 9 warp threads and weave the design shown to $2\frac{3}{4}$ ins. If finger is large, weave 2 or 3 extra rows between fishes in order to extend it. Add fringing if required. (In chart above: o=yellow, x=blue.)

Take ring off loom and tie the corresponding ends of warp threads together to form a ring shape.

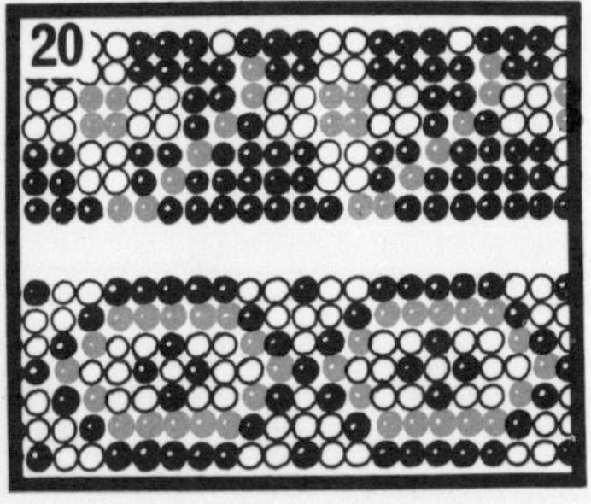

Use the methods described to make other bead bracelets, necklaces, rings, belts, etc.

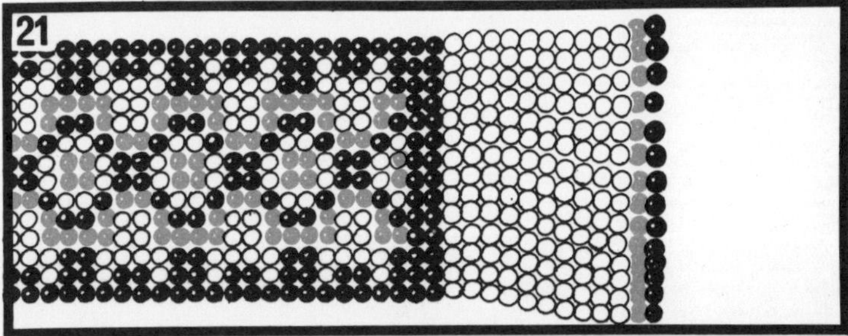

If weaving a belt, add a fringe at the ends by taking warp threads off singly when design is finished and threading 10 or more beads on each one. Take thread round last bead, thread up through fringe and into main bead row as for side fringes.

Stringing Along

String pictures are equally effective for representational, figurative or abstract designs. They are fascinating to make, allowing great scope for invention, combining as they do both graphic and sculptural effects. When hung they respond to subtle lighting. The design here has been called 'Salome' as it gives the effect of floating veils.

YOU WILL NEED:
Piece of plywood or chipboard, 15×12 ins.
Piece of velvet finish self-adhesive film, 18×18 ins.
Supply of flat-headed $\frac{3}{4}$ in. nails, about 1/16 in. thick
1 spool of black, 1 spool of white gimp thread
Light hammer · scissors ruler
Pencil

Cut the plywood or board to size and smooth and finish the edges with coarse and then fine sand-paper.

Lay the board on a larger sheet of paper and draw round the edge of the board on the paper.

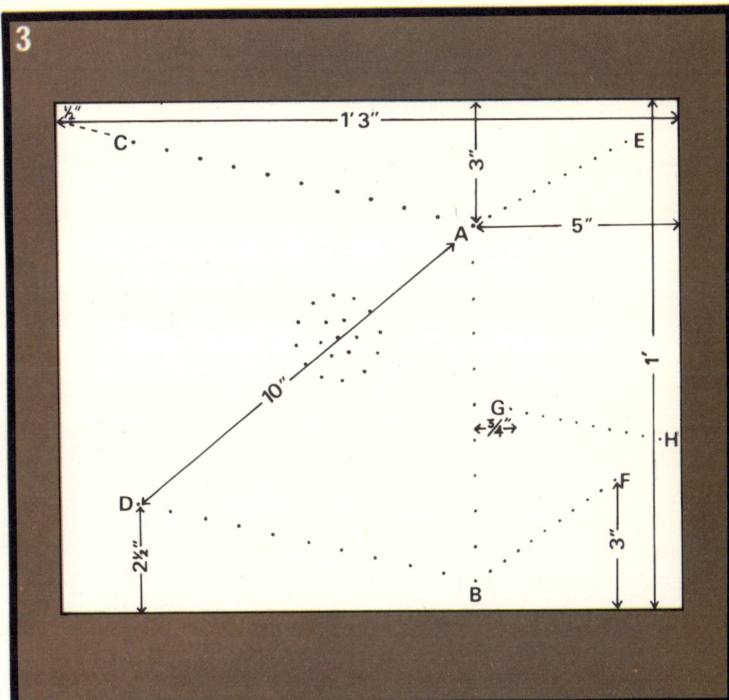

In pencil, mark position of nails on paper. Mark point A 3 ins. from top, 5 ins. from right and draw in lines AB, AC, AE and BD, BF and GH. Draw circular motif as shown. AB, AC and BD nails should be $\frac{3}{4}$ in. apart; all others $\frac{3}{8}$ in. apart.

Cut velvet film $1\frac{1}{2}$ ins. larger all round than board, mitre corners, peel off backing, stick firmly down on the board.

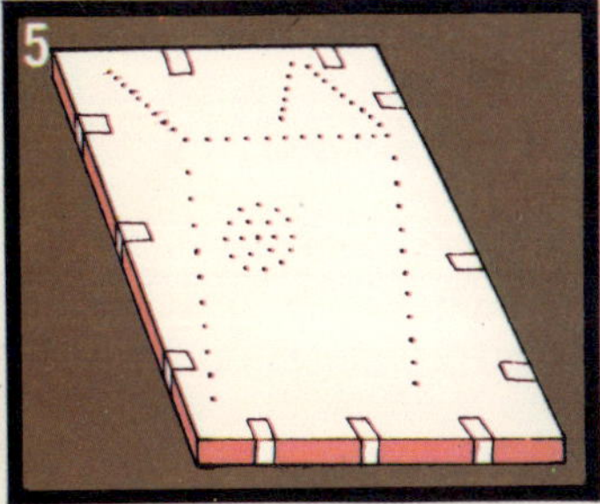

Lay paper nailing plan down on board and stick over edges and down back with tape. This will be removed later.

Now hammer in nails on points you have marked through paper, being careful to leave just over $\frac{1}{2}$ in. of nail shank showing. Make sure nails are vertical, parallel and evenly spaced or picture will be inaccurate. Tear off paper.

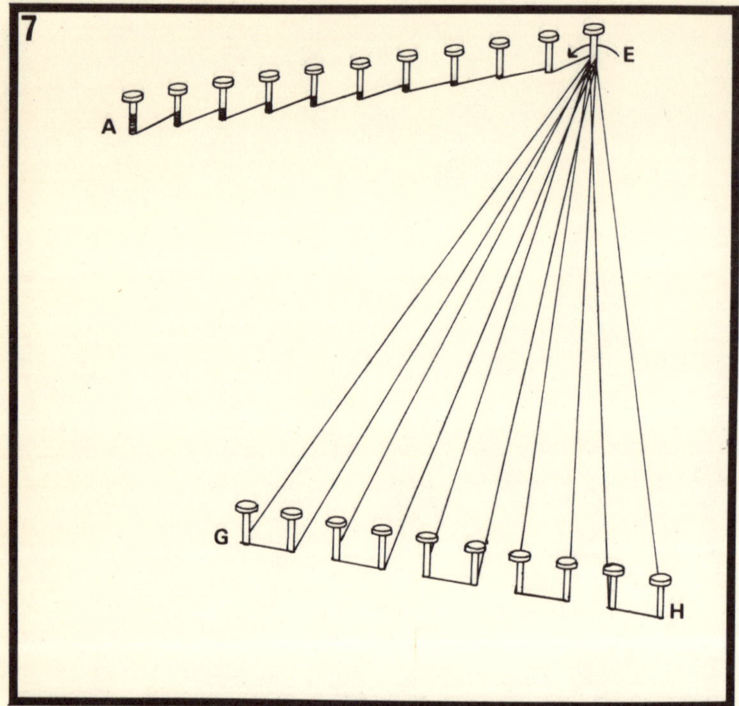

Tie black thread to E, then wind string in EHG pattern as shown. Next take thread from E to A round nails, steadily increasing number of turns round each nail to raise centre of design. Attach white thread at C and do likewise from C to A.

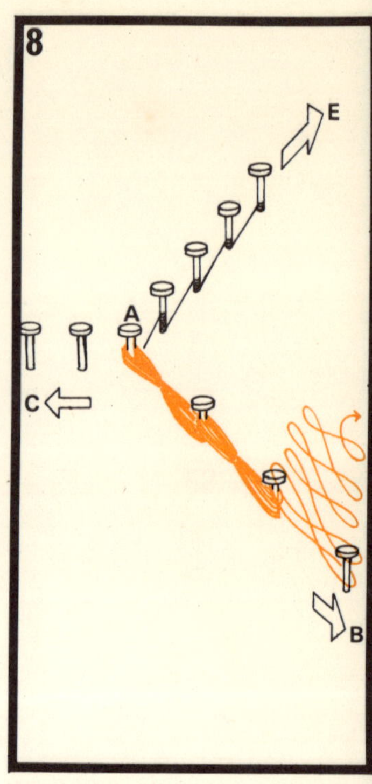

Wind white thread in small criss-cross hanks down centre column from A to B, making a winding pattern as shown.

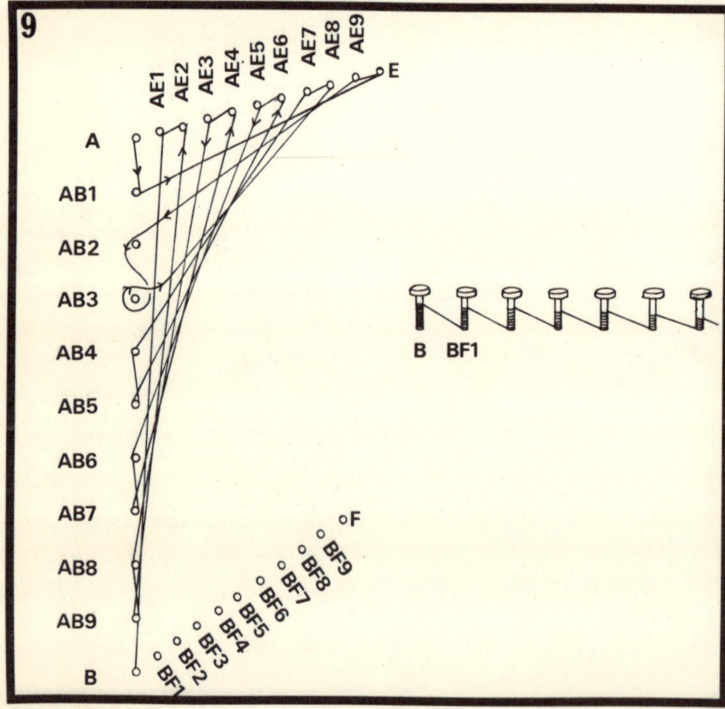

Take black thread round under head of A, then round AB1 next round E and AE9, (in that order); then round AB2 and AB3, then AE8 and AE7, and so on. Next wind 10 times round B, 9 times round BF1 and so on to F, reducing turns as you progress.

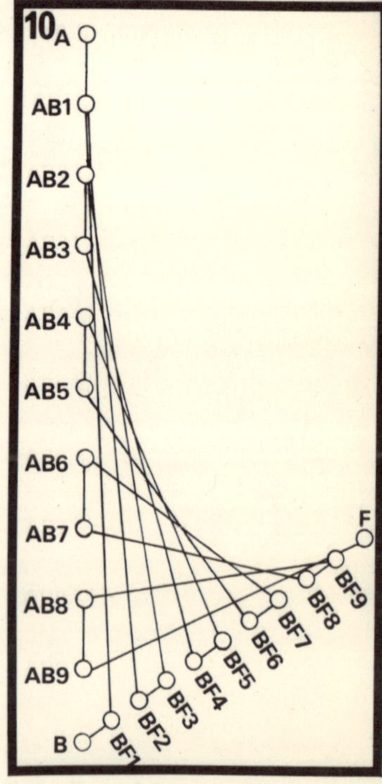

From F work round AB9 and AB8, back to BF9 and BF8, then to BF7, BF6, AB7 and AB6 etc., back to A and tie off.

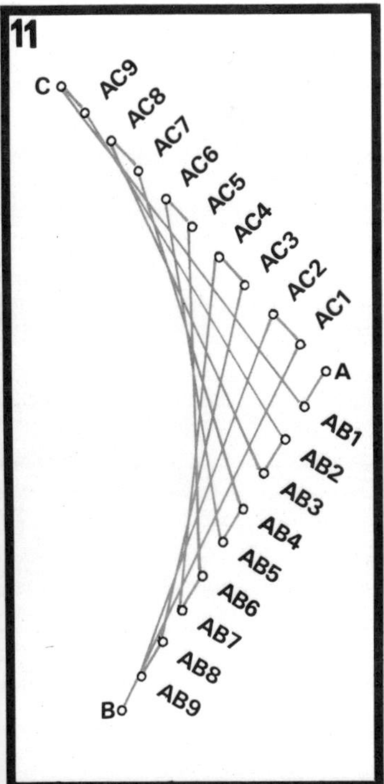

Take white thread round head of B to AC1, AC2 to AB9, AB8, then to AC3, AC4 and so on up to C exactly as for black thread.

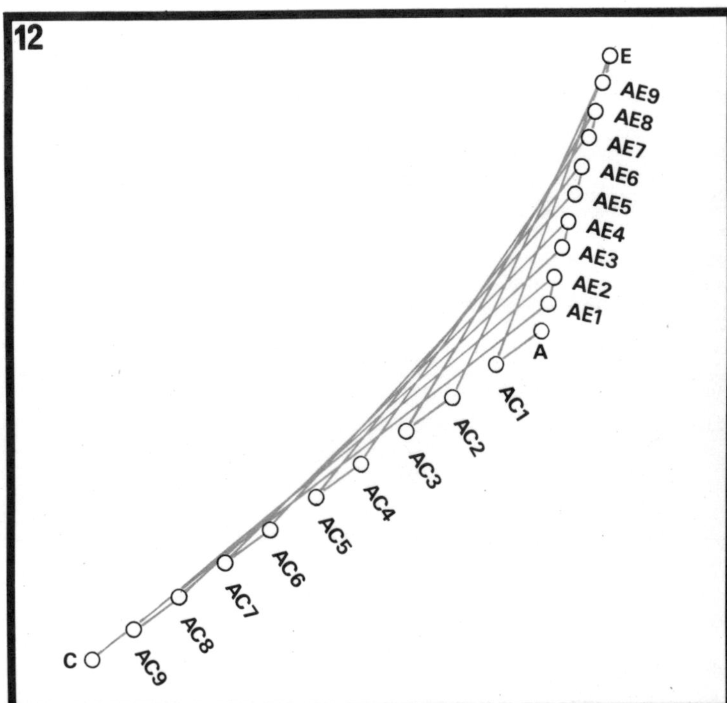

The upper mesh CAE is strung on in white as shown, in exactly the same way as the CAB stringing. When completed, finish off the loose thread with a neat knot. This completes the main design.

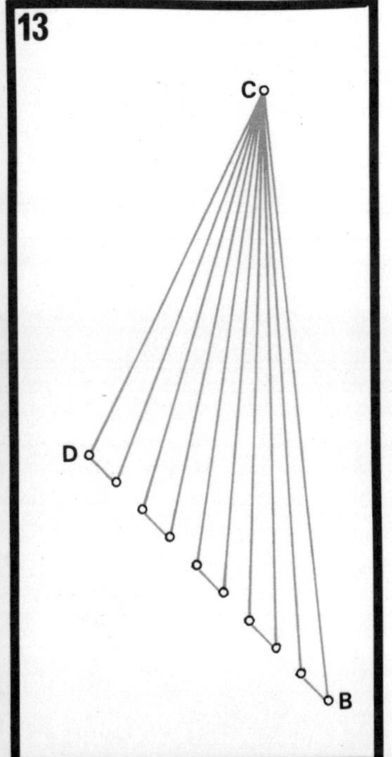

Now work a stringing pattern (CBD1D) in white exactly as for pattern EHG, (see note 7) ending at C.

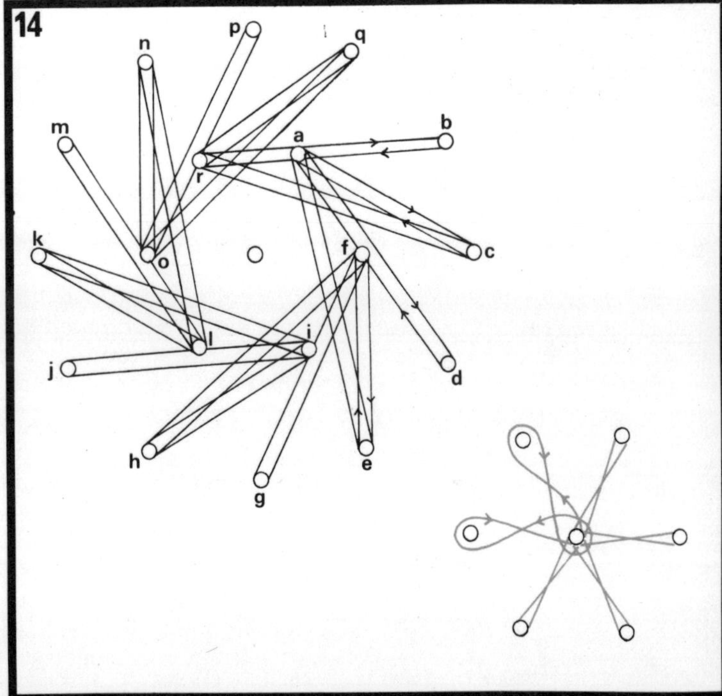

For circular motif, wind black threads in clockwise turns from a round b, back to a, aca, ada, aef; repeat with f as base, going round e, g, h, ending at i, which becomes next base and so on. Work asterisk pattern in white round 7 inside nails.

Coat Of Paint

Leather and suede gifts are really luxurious—yet even a bag or tunic bought from the most home-spun craft shop lacks the personal touch which really 'makes' a gift. Here's a way to add that special something to a leather or suede bag or tunic—paint a design on it! Using a suede dye, it's possible to achieve lovely colour effects, with the advantage that the garment may be dry-cleaned later. If the leather or suede is washable, the garment may still be washed after it's been painted, using a mild soap liquid or leather shampoo. Before you begin your painting give the item a thorough clean with a reliable suede cleaner. And don't forget, the same treatment can do wonders for an article that has done the rounds and is beginning to look a bit drab. This way you can give any kind of not-so-new leather or suede a new lease of life!

YOU WILL NEED:
Plain leather waistcoat
Suede dyes in 5 colours
Small art brush
Suede brush
Soft pencil

Trace the flower and bud shapes shown above on to a sheet of stiff card, then cut them out to form a stencil. The flower stamens and stalks may be painted in freehand, but if you are not an experienced artist, practise first on a piece of paper.

Using a soft pencil, lightly draw in the 'plant pot' (if no pocket) and stems. Stencil in flower shapes in pencil.

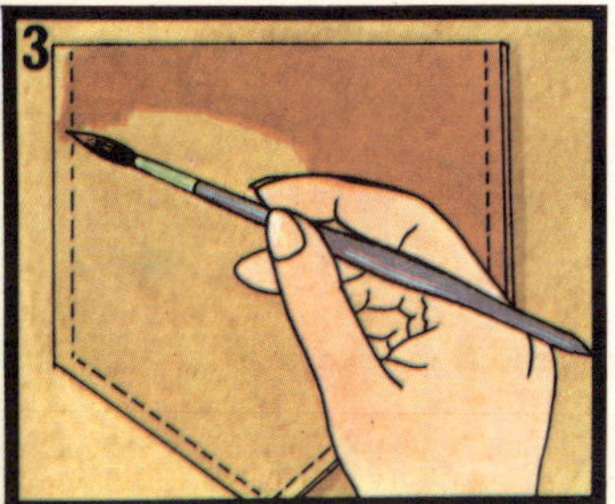

Shake dye, then paint 'pot', allow to dry, and brush to bring up nap. Repaint to deepen colour: brush again.

Rinse and dry paintbrush. Paint stems and stalks in green, following pencil outline. Allow to dry repeat colour and brushing.

Paint in solid purple petals. The flowers should be graded in size, the smaller ones coming at top of design.

Repeat colouring over purple petals; allow this strong colour to dry thoroughly before brushing with suede brush.

Paint freehand the seven-coloured stamens on each flower. Make top part of each wider than bottom.

If liked, draw a matching design on the back of the waistcoat and paint in colours as above.

Roll Out That Vase!

Who ever would have thought that making a clay vase could be as easy as rolling pastry? But it is . . . if you follow the instructions here to make this very attractive gift. Choose one of the self-hardening modelling clays, which, when dry, have the strength of ceramics but are less fragile. The clay dries with very little shrinkage and does not need firing. Decorations can be added in a variety of ways: shapes cut from clay slabs can be applied; coins, butter markers and leaves can be impressed into the drying clay, and so on. Paint the vase with poster paint when it is completely dry, choosing bright or subtle colours. Allow to dry again and then apply a coat of varnish. You can vary the design by covering the plastic bottle with a sheet of clay, stitching the single join; or you can make a set of three vases in graded sizes as a very special gift.

YOU WILL NEED:
Self-hardening modelling clay
Used plastic bottle
Newspaper
Short length of $\frac{1}{4}$ in. batten
Rolling pin
Craft knife · blunt edged tool
Ruler · stiff paper or card
Pencil · poster paint
Varnish · paintbrush

To give stability to the vase, use a cylindrical plastic bottle, such as one which has held washing-up liquid. Any size will do. Using a thick wad of newspaper as a base and $\frac{1}{4}$ in. battens as guides, roll out 4 pieces of clay for the sides of the vase.

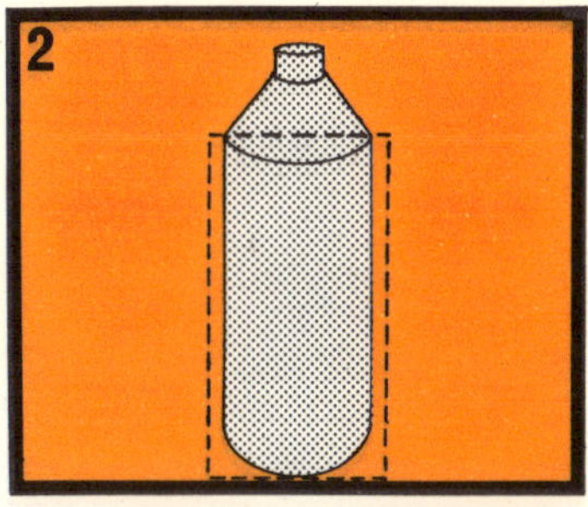

Each piece of clay should be 1 in. wider than the diameter of the bottle and $1\frac{1}{2}$ ins. shorter than the height.

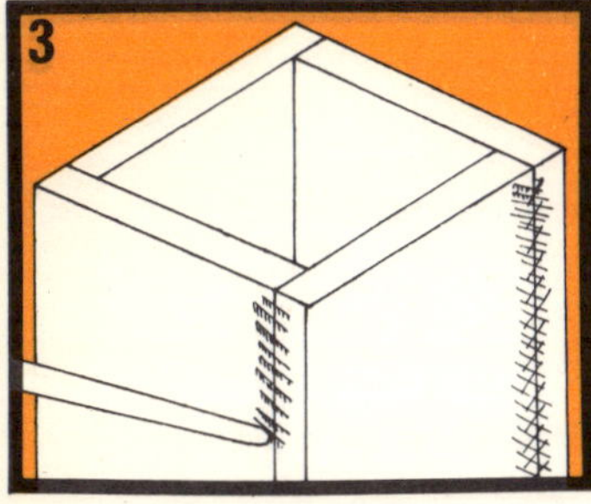

Cut pieces accurately; dampen edges and then 'stitch' each join with criss-cross marks; using a blunt-ended tool.

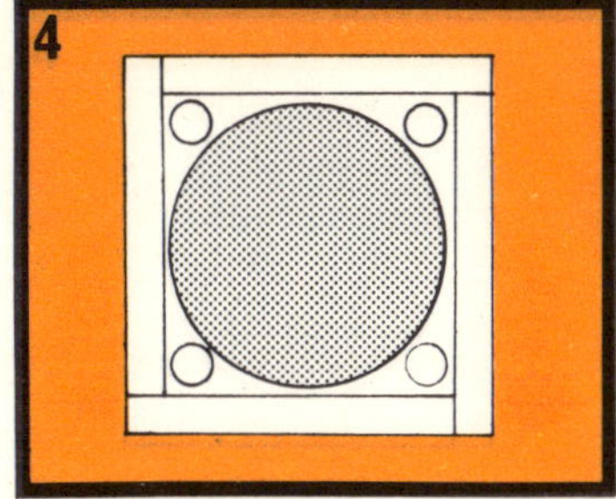

Keep the shape rigid by rolling up tight wads of newspaper, standing 1 at each corner between bottle and clay.

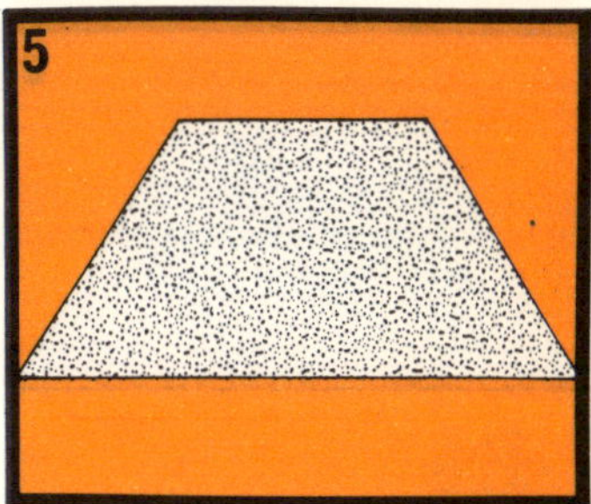

Leave to dry. Cut pattern for the sloping top pieces, the width of the vase wide, half this in depth and at top edge.

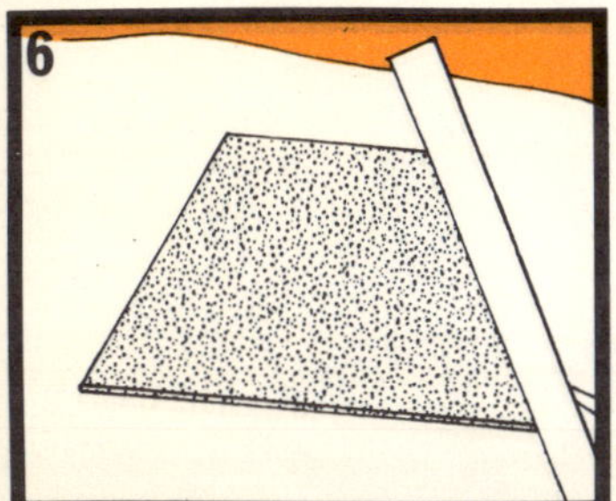

Cut pattern in stiff paper or card and use to cut 4 identical clay pieces. These should be $\frac{1}{4}$ in. thick.

Cut small piece of clay from inner edges of the 4 pieces before adding them to the top. Smooth and score each piece.

Wrap small collar of newspaper round top of bottle to help hold the sloping sides in place while they dry.

Cut piece of clay overlapping top to hide top of bottle. If necessary, trim piece from container. Again stitch joins.

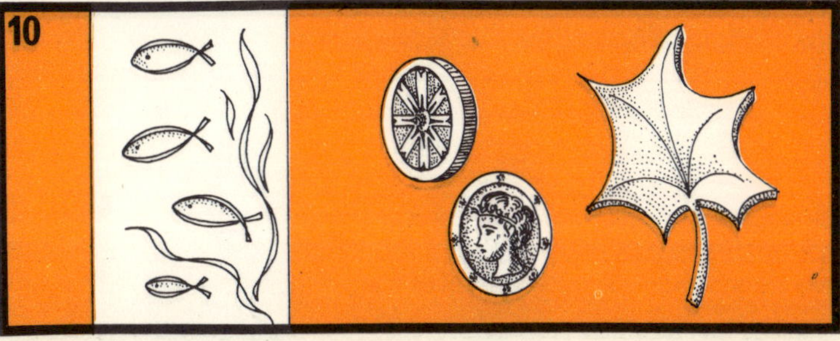

To decorate the vase, cut shapes from $\frac{1}{8}$ in. thick pieces of clay, dampen and press into the sides; or impress shapes from thick card cut-outs. Remove paper and bottle while vase dries. If it shrinks, trim inside. Replace bottle. Paint and gloss to finish.

Owl Shoulder Bag

Any teenage girl would love this crazy owl shoulder bag with its huge brown eyes and mottled feather body. Give it a strong cotton lining, unless it is to carry just books and college papers.

Only two colours of dye and a household bleach produce the colour variations. To prepare string for dyeing measure it and wind it into loose skeins. Wash well in hot water and detergent. Rinse and then dye while wet. Dye 140 yards of fillis twine in dark brown. Then dye another 100 yards medium brown by putting it in the same dye bath where the colour will have become weaker. Dye the parcel twine in this, too. Then dye 50 yards fillis twine in gold, and bleach another 50 yards fillis in strong bleach and water solution until it starts to lighten. Rinse all twine well and hang in sun, if possible, to dry.

YOU WILL NEED:
3 1-lb. balls of 4 or 5 ply fillis garden twine
Multi-purpose dye in gold and brown
Household bleach
About 8 yds heavy white parcel twine
Scissors · long pins
Working surface, about 18 ins. square
Old foam cushion or soft wallboard

In Instructions:
DHH=Double Half Hitch
VDHH=Vertical Double Half Hitch
DDHH=Diagonal Double Half Hitch
HHH=Horizontal Half Hitch
HDHH=Horizontal Double Half Hitch

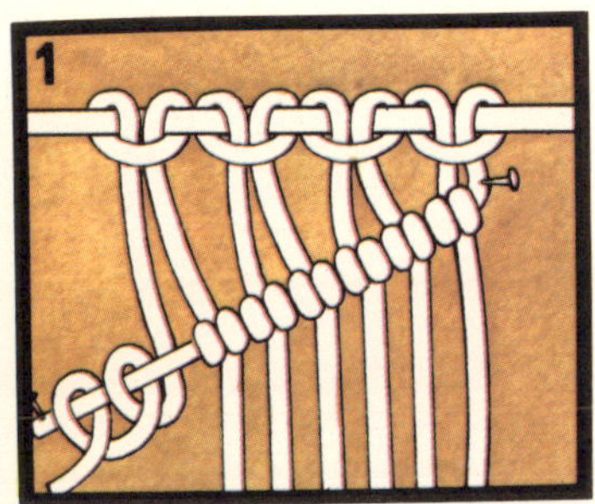

Diagonal Half-Hitch, used in the bag, is worked like the Horizontal version, except for the angle of knot-bearing cord.

In the vertical Double Half Hitch, also used, the same cord, (either first or last in row), is knotted across each of the others in turn. When one row has been completed, the cord travels back in the opposite direction, below the first row.

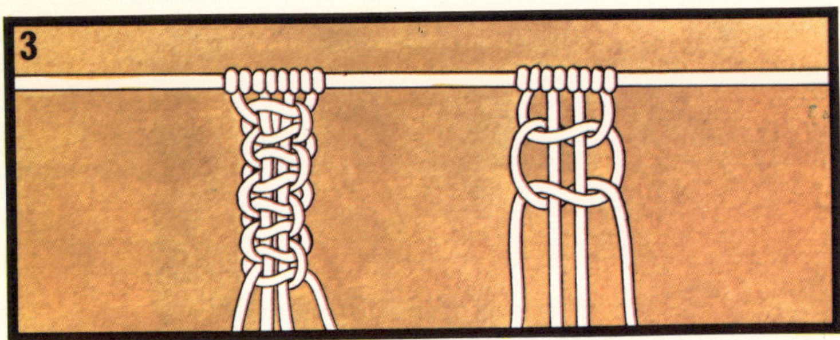

The Flat Knot also used is a reef knot, which can be tied over 2 or more filler cords. Cord 1 travels over, and cord 4 under cords 2 and 3, and out through loops. Cord 1 travels back over and cord 4 back under 2 filler cords, and through loops.

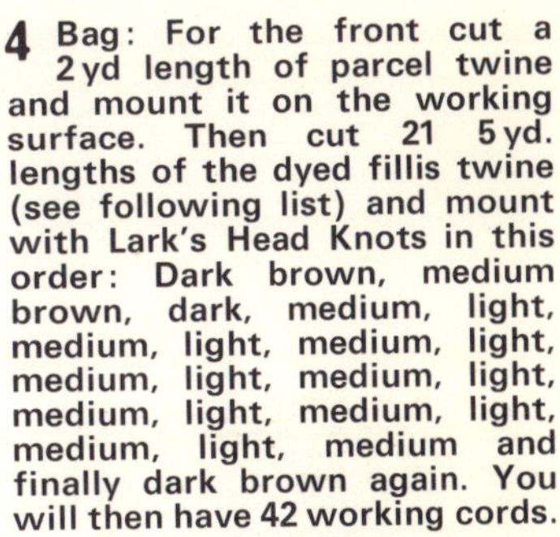

4 Bag: For the front cut a 2 yd length of parcel twine and mount it on the working surface. Then cut 21 5 yd. lengths of the dyed fillis twine (see following list) and mount with Lark's Head Knots in this order: Dark brown, medium brown, dark, medium, light, medium, light, medium, light, medium, light, medium, light, medium, light, medium, light, medium, light, medium and finally dark brown again. You will then have 42 working cords.

Make a row of Alternating Flat Knots—tie cords 1 and 4 over 2 and 3; 5 and 8 over 6 and 7 and so on. *Next row:* leave cords 1 and 2 inactive, knot cords 3 and 6 over 4 and 5; knot 7 and 10 over 8 and 9, and so on, leaving aside last two.

6 Follow the Alternating Knot pattern shown on the left. Begin in the middle of the row by tying 2 light cords over 2 medium brown ones. Work across the row first out to one side and then to the other. At the edges, include the parcel twine, making it the second cord in from the edge. This cord is always the filler cord and is there to strengthen the edges. To continue the alternating pattern in the second row, you must tie the brown cords over the light ones. This completes the striped pattern.

Work pattern for 10 rows. Add 2 more 5 yd. lengths of dark brown by tying a Flat Knot round last 2 cords at each end.

Adjust strings so parcel twine is still second from edge, i.e.: the filler cord—and is not used for tying.

Knot 10 rows, add 2 5 yd. lengths, knot until 11 ins. Decrease one knot each end to point. With 2 outside cords, tie VDHH over each cord.

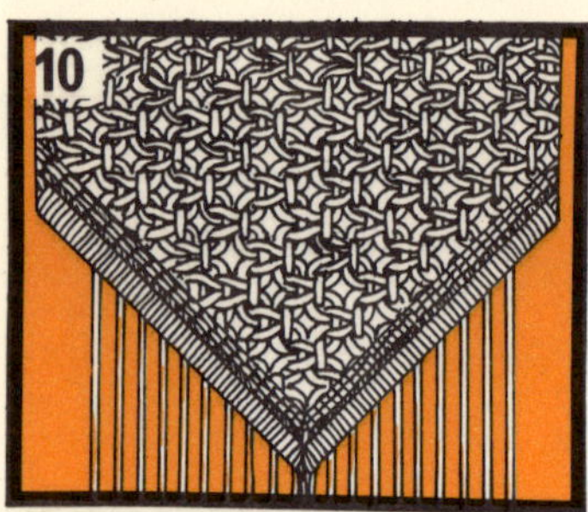

10

With outside cords as leaders, tie DDHH to point. With 2nd cord as leader, tie one VDHH over it with outside cord to give stitching line.

11

Using both cords as leaders, tie a DDHH over them. Then use all 3 cords as leaders and knot a DDHH with 4th cord.

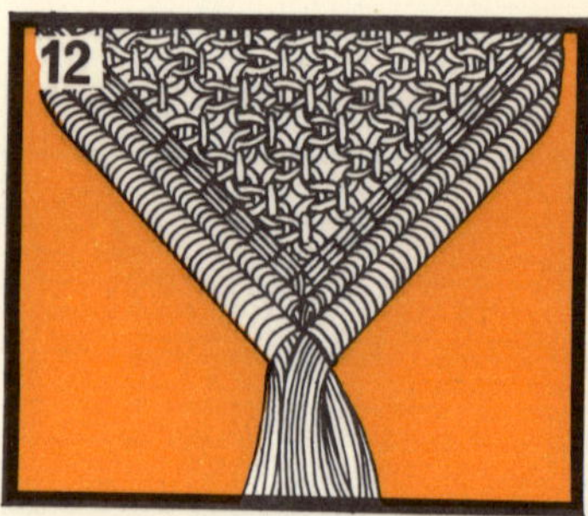

12

Knot over all cords with 5th cord; add each knotting cord to leaders down to point. This completes front. Join cords for tail.

13 Front flap and back, begin with beak and work upside down over back to tail. Cut a piece of parcel twine 2½ yds. long and pin a short inverted V shape in the middle. Cut 4 lengths, each 6 yds. long of gold, and mount 2 on each side of beak, using Lark's Head Knots. Work one Half-Hitch on each side of each knot to fill in the spaces and make a firmer edge. You have 8 knotting cords facing each other on 2 sides of a square. Work Double Half-Hitches over them all in turn with all the others until you have worked a square.

14 Work 2 rows of DHH; use outside cords as leaders and bringing them to a point. Leave aside the 2 outside leaders and work another row towards the point, with 6 cords. Leave aside 2 outside cords and work towards the point with 4 cords. Repeat this step. You will now have reached the tip of the beak. Turn the work over so that the "wrong side" is facing you. Cut 10 dark brown cords and mount them–5 on either side of the beak–on the parcel twine. Work an extra Half-Hitch on either side of each Lark's Head to strengthen the edge.

15 Cut 24 yd. length of medium brown and pin in middle under the beak. Work DHH over the 10 dark brown cords cut from the centre and then back towards the centre. Be sure to knot over the heavy string at the outside edges. Cross string over, under beak, to hold it in place. Knot over first gold cord from the beak. Knot VDHH over only 4 cords and turn back to centre. Cross over, under beak again, and include second gold cord.

16

Now lay bangles in place on either side of the beak and work 3 HH with each of the centre 6 dark brown cords for each eye.

17

Cut 2 6 yd. lengths of dark brown. Mount on each outer edge, just inside edging cord, by looping through the above VDHH.

18

Cut 2 7 yd. lengths of medium brown and pin 1 at top centre of each bangle. Fill in round outside top quarter of bangle with VDHH.

19 As you do this, work 3 HH over the outside quarter of bangle with the next 4 dark brown cords. Work VDHH over last 2 cords and heavy edging cord *half-way* down bangle. You must now fill in the eye with gold. Cut two 6 yd. lengths of gold and pin in place at top of bangle under work. Now work VDHH back and forth over the dark brown cords as tightly as possible. It may be easier to fill in evenly with a single Half Hitch in the curve. Work a little on each eye at a time to keep the work even.

20 When in middle, work 2 brown HHH over 2 middle gold cords. For the next row, work 4 HDHH and 2 in the next row, filling in with gold VDHH all round. Finish with gold cords at bottom of the eye. Cover rest of bangle with 3 Half-Hitches using each of the dark brown cords. Leave gold cord lying underneath at this point. Go back to the middle below the beak and continue filling in between the eyes with medium brown cords there. Be sure to work over all the gold cords and continue crossing over, under the beak.

21 At bottom of beak, (you are working upside down), combine the last 2 gold cords with the 2 before, so that you are knotting over 2 cords in just the centre 2 knots. This helps to reduce the bulk. Work a solid curved area of medium brown under the eyes. You will have 4 knottings cords. Be sure to twist the cords around each other where they meet to prevent holes in the work. Do not cut them off –you will soon need them as knotting cords. With 2 of the middle gold cords, work a curved row of VDHH out from the centre over all cords to define edge of eye area. These cords now lie at outer edges, outside edging cord.

Cut 2 4 yd. lengths of dark brown. Add inside outer edge by tying a Flat Knot around last 2 cords from edge.

From centre of curved area, work Alt. Flat knots for 15 rows. Add 2 4 yd. lengths med. brown, keeping heavy cord second from end.

Work 6 ins. and add another 4 yd. length of medium brown in the same way. Continue until work measures 15 ins.

Finish as for front, tapering first to a point. Then work a row of VDHH, and 2 rows of cording. (See front.)

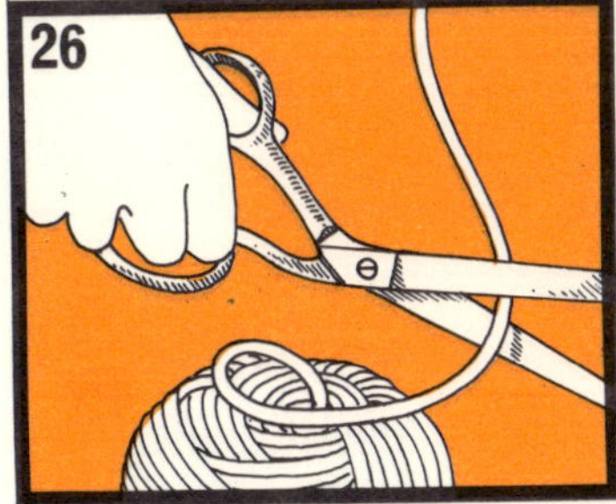

For gusset and handle, cut 3 yd. length parcel twine; fold in half. Cut 10 yd. lengths of lightest colour, gold and dark brown.

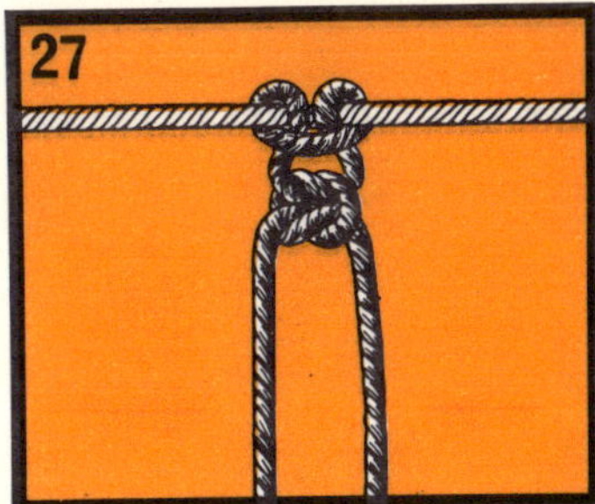

Mount dark brown in the middle of parcel twine. Tie one Flat knot with *just* brown cord to fill in tapered point of gusset.

Mount gold and light cords each side of brown. Work Alt. Flat knot for 50 ins. Bring heavy cord to middle, knot over it with others.

To join: place front on back and sew up from point between 2 rows of cording. Use a blunt-pointed needle and stab stitch.

Lay gusset in place on side and sew firmly through heavy cord on both pieces. Make stitches at top especially strong.

Use a large, blunt-pointed needle to thread in ends on back of flap. Trim ends close to work and cut to neaten.

Wrap all cords together, wrap 2 dark brown ones round others. Tighten 2 ends, flatten coil. Trim fringe so ends taper to point.

This diagram shows how a coil is wrapped. The method is used for tassels on wallhangings, curtain ties and sash belts.

Cube Clock

Finding something for the infamous 'man who has everything' can often be a problem. Yet the novel gift shown here—the cube clock—might well prove to be just the answer. Cube clocks are expensive to buy, but the one shown here is a very attractive and easy-to-make version that won't be too much of a blow to the purse. On top of that, it has the added advantage of being 'personalised' by the inclusion of photographs, holiday snapshots and postcards—if you wish. Of course the natty little cube clock isn't only for that difficult man—it'll go down just as well with a teenage girl (for her bedroom), that far-away sister or cousin—and even with Gran . . . just right for the mantelpiece!

YOU WILL NEED:
Perspex photograph cube, approx. $3\frac{1}{2} \times 3\frac{1}{2} \times 3\frac{1}{2}$ ins. with open back and complete with foam cube
Small clock without legs which is adjustable at back and which will fit into cube with comfortable margin
Stiff coloured paper or card
Coloured photographs, holiday snapshots or postcards slightly larger or same size as cube sides

Remove foam cube from perspex and place clock face down centrally on one of its sides. Draw round face with felt-tip.

Using a saw-edged knife, carefully hollow out the foam in a circle to the depth of the clock, leaving edges intact.

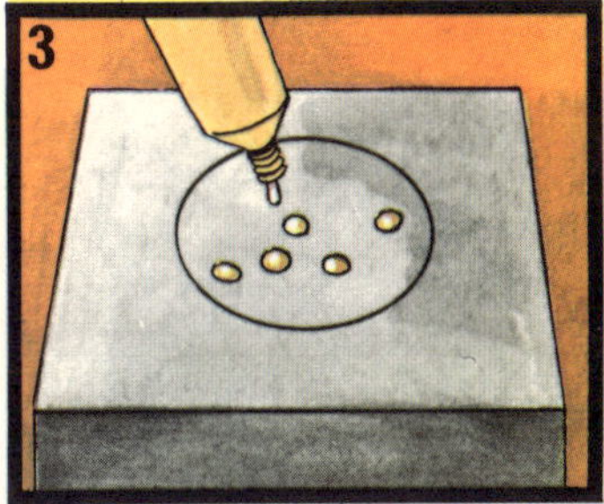

Alternatively, soften the foam with solvent, such as acetone, where it is to be removed; scoop out with an old spoon.

Fit the clock in hole in cube so that clock face is level with foam edge. It should be snug but not too tight.

The clock is now held in position by the foam and may be inserted in perspex cube. It can be withdrawn for winding.

Cut out three photographs, postcards or pieces of coloured card to the exact internal size of perspex sides.

Slip foam and clock in cube and slide in photos or card at sides and top, trimming if necessary to make them fit exactly.

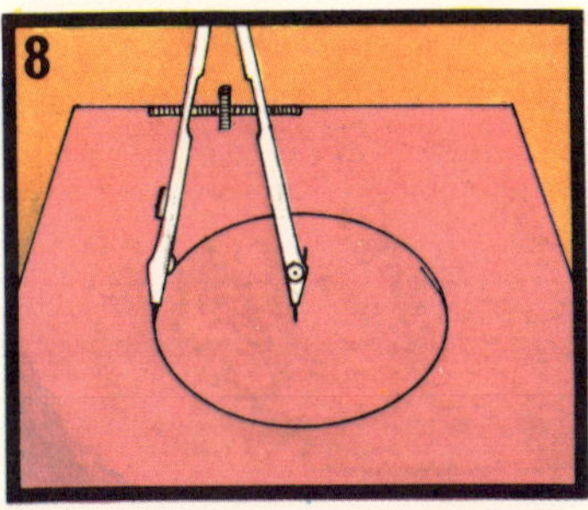

Cut a piece of coloured card the size of perspex side, and with compasses draw a circle, clock face size, in the middle.

Cut out circle very carefully, using small sharp scissors or a cutting blade which fits in the compasses.

Remove clock, foam and pictures from cube and insert card with circle cut out in face opposite opening. Trim if necessary.

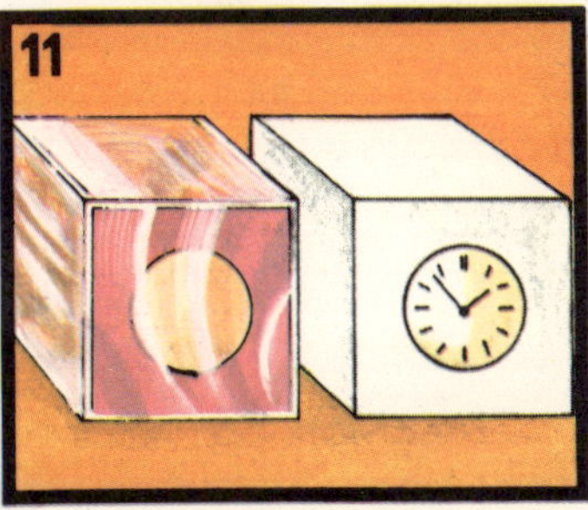

Carefully insert the foam cube and wound clock, pushing up so that the face shows through the hole in the coloured card.

Insert pictures or plain coloured card pieces in the top and sides of the cubes to complete the clock.

Polar Family

And finally, a gift for everyone! Enchanting, fluffy white polar bears—easy to make, charming to look at, especially super to cuddle. They are a natural present to give a small child, either as a pair or just one on its own, and an older child will love them too as a shelf or bedroom ornament. There are even a lot of grown-ups we know, who have never quite lost their 'penchant' for soft, cuddly toys. As gifts then, these polar bears will be real winners—the only trouble being that once your friends or young relatives have seen them, you could find yourself inundated with orders!

YOU WILL NEED:
1 yd. 36 in. wide white fluffy Courtelle or similar fabric
Matching sewing thread
Scissors · Needle and pins
Stuffing, such as Kapok
Black buttons or black embroidery thread

PATTERN FOR POLAR BEAR Each square = 1 in.

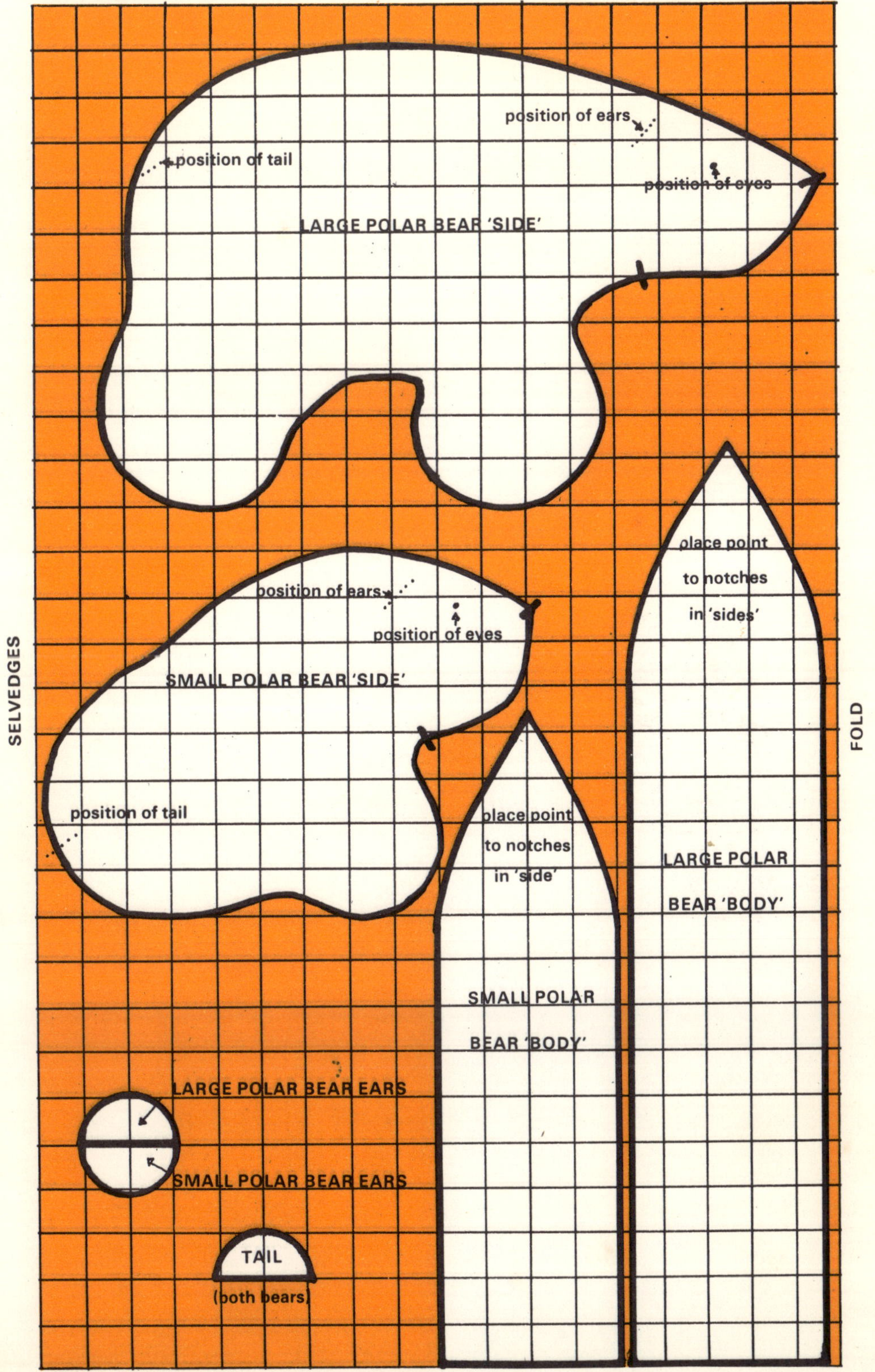

Above are the pattern pieces for both polar bears. Each square on the patterns equals 1 in. on the models. Transfer the pattern pieces to dressmaker's squared paper upgrading the size to this ratio. Cut out the paper patterns and place them on folded fabric as indicated by above layout. Pin through both layers of fabric and cut out so you have two fabric shapes of each piece.

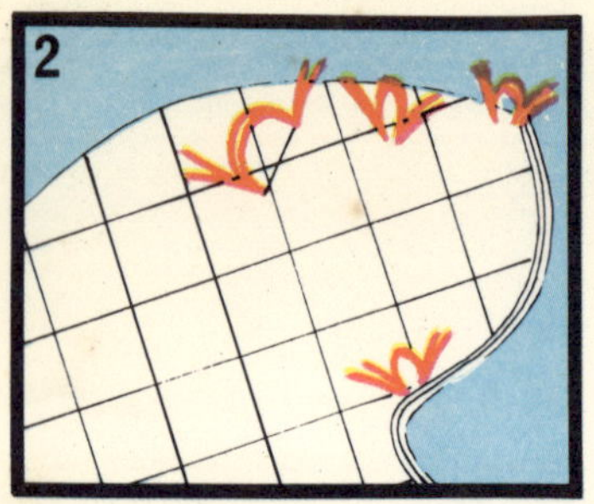

Transfer notches at 'nose' and neck, and position of ears, eyes and tails paper from pattern to fabric pieces with tailor's tacks.

Remove paper patterns from fabric shapes. Keep for use again.

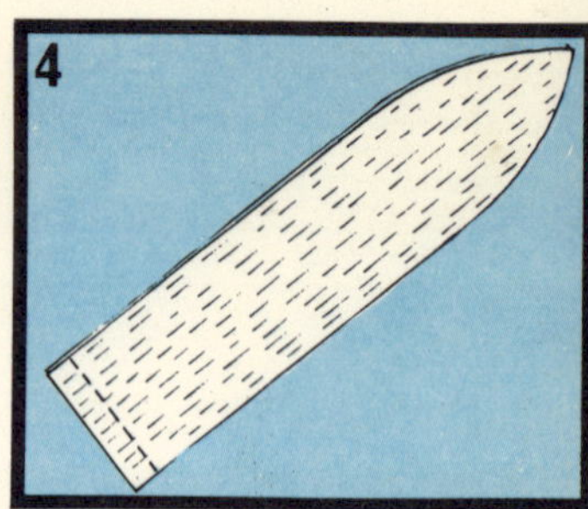

Right sides of fabric together, pin and stitch along short straight edges of both bear 'body' pieces, allowing ½ in. on seams.

Right sides of fabric together, pin and tack large bear 'side' pieces to either side of 'body' strip allowing ½ in. seam turnings. Point of body strip should line up with notches at nose and under neck.

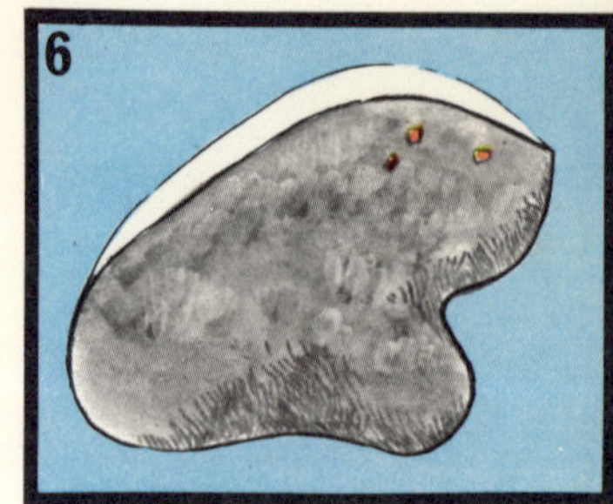

Stitch in place and do the same with the small polar bear side and body pieces. Turn to right side.

Stuff both bears firmly through 'neck to nose' opening. Sew up openings using small firm oversewing stitches.

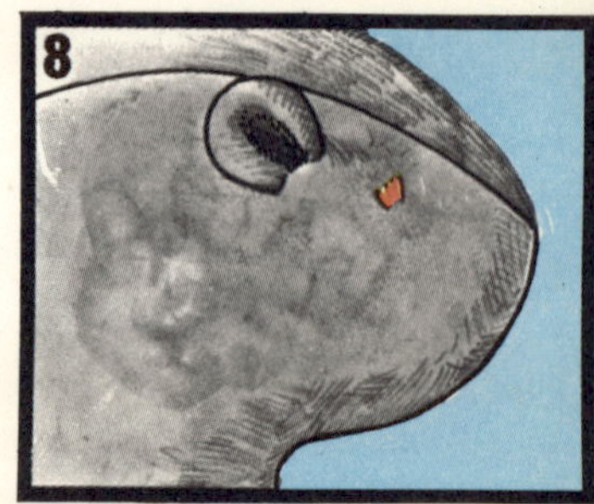

Make a small pleat in ear pieces and sew to polar bears in positions marked using small oversewing stitches.

Make a small pleat in the tail pieces and sew these on in the same way to positions marked.

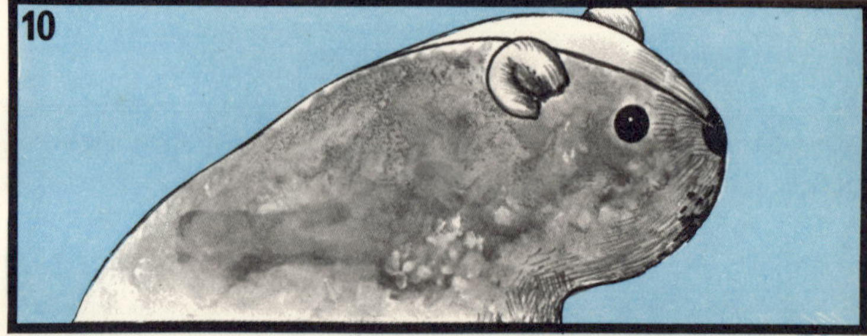

Sew on buttons for ears and eyes in marked positions. Alternatively embroider features using black thread and satin stitch.